Unfinished

A Christian Story of Fatherhood, Faith, and the Grace That Stayed.

By

Dr. Ty H. Wenglar

Email: ty@wenglargroup.com
Phone: 832-256-9669
www.tywenglar.com | www.lucentraadvisors.com | www.empowermentrwanda.org

LIMITS OF LIABILITY / DISCLAIMER OF WARRANTY:

The author and publisher of this book have used their best efforts in preparing this material. While every attempt has been made to verify information provided in this book, neither the author nor the publisher assumes any responsibility for any errors, omissions, or inaccuracies.

The author and publisher make no representation or warranties with respect to the accuracy, applicability, fitness, or completeness of the contents of this program. They disclaim any warranties (expressed or implied), merchantability, or fitness for any purpose. The author and publisher shall in no event be held liable for any loss or other damages, including but not limited to special, incidental, consequential, or other damages. As always, the advice of a competent legal, tax, accounting or other professional should be sought.

THE LIONFISH PRESS

Acknowledgments

To my parents, Buck and Lisa Wenglar and Sandi Richards, who planted the seeds of curiosity and love for learning in me. Thank you for teaching me the value of education and for being my constant source of motivation and encouragement.

In the loving memory of my grandmother, Myrtle "Totsie" Wenglar, whose support and belief in my potential were unwavering.

Dedication

To my beloved wife.

Cathy, you have been my rock, enduring the long hours and absences, managing our household, caring for our children with unwavering dedication, and ensuring our home was a place of peace and progress. Your ability to juggle countless responsibilities while being my steadfast supporter is nothing short of miraculous. I am forever grateful for your love, patience, and sacrifice.

I didn't plan to write this book. It wasn't in the career folder or tucked inside some long-held dream. There was no five-year vision, no book proposal, no polished idea I carried in my back pocket. I wasn't looking to become a writer.

I was just trying to make it through daily life.

Trying to keep my marriage together.

Trying to pray, or at least not curse God out loud in the dark.

Trying to raise kids who wouldn't grow up haunted by the same silence I was choking on.

And then grace started tapping on my shoulder.

Not the sweet, polite kind you put on a coffee mug. Not the feel-good kind you find in Sunday school illustrations. The kind that doesn't knock...it kicks the door off its hinges and sits beside you in the wreckage.

I've seen that kind of grace. In warzones and in bedrooms. In VA waiting rooms and kitchen tables. In the eyes of my children who didn't ask for a broken father, and the quiet strength of a wife who kept loving me when I didn't have anything left to give back.

This isn't a theology book. I'm not a priest. I'm not a scholar. Some days, I don't even know if I'd make a very good Catholic. But grace didn't wait for me to be impressive. It just stayed. And when it stayed long enough, I realized I couldn't keep quiet anymore.

So I wrote.

I wrote because I've sat in too many rooms with men who think they're the only ones unraveling. I wrote because I've stared at too many ceilings asking questions that never got answers...but somehow, grace came anyway. I wrote because maybe somebody needs to know they're not disqualified by their scars. That grace doesn't need you to be cleaned up. It just needs you to say yes.

This book is not a clean arc from trauma to triumph. It's not a memoir about winning. It's a witness to staying. To choosing to believe that even if your story doesn't make sense yet, God is still in it. That grace is not just what saves you...it's what stays with you.

I didn't set out to write this.

But grace set out to find me.

And now you're holding the evidence in your hands.

This isn't a theology book and it's not a memoir either.

What you're holding is a conversation between a former construction executive and then combat medic and anyone who's ever wondered why they're still here, why others didn't make it, and how grace could possibly be enough to make sense of it all.

I didn't set out to write a book. I was sitting in Mass on Easter Sunday when the word *grace* just wouldn't leave me alone. The memory of a song. The weight of things I've carried. The slow, steady realization that grace had met me in every chapter, even the ones I wouldn't have chosen.

So this book isn't a performance. It's a witness.

I'm not writing as someone who has all the answers. I'm writing as someone who's seen just enough grace to believe it's worth handing on.

You'll hear stories of war, from wounds, from family life, and from the silence after the adrenaline fades. But more than that, I hope you'll hear an invitation...not to figure it out, but to see your own life with new eyes.

Here's how I hope you'll read this:

- Slowly. There's no rush.
- Honestly. Let the stories echo your own.
- Reflectively. Bring a journal or a friend. Some parts are better processed in company.
- Openly. Not to my story, but to the grace that's been chasing yours.

Whether you're reading this alone, in a small group, or somewhere in between deployments, my prayer is simple:

That you'd see again. That you'd name grace where it's been all along. And that you'd never mistake survival for the end of your story.

You're still here for a reason.
Let's find out why.

...Ty

Part 1: Easter Mass, the Word That Cut Through

I hadn't planned on writing anything that morning. I hadn't even planned on thinking deeply. It was Easter Sunday...one of those high holy days where Christians, Catholic or Protestant, regardless of how long they've been away, find themselves back in the pews. The church was packed, predictably so. People filled every row in front of me, behind me, all around me. Children squirmed in dress clothes, mothers gave tight smiles, fathers stood stoic. The usual smells of incense hung in the air, mingling with wax, perfume, and something else I still can't name. Something sacred. Something that doesn't smell like anything else until you've smelled it in that setting…timeless, ancient, unsettling.

I was sitting there, just another man in the pews. On the outside, I looked like anyone else, another husband, another father, another Catholic doing his holy-day duty. But internally, I was far from calm. My head was buzzing, not with noise, exactly, but with a kind of spiritual static. Not anger. Not peace. Just... distance. I stood when I was supposed to, knelt at the right times, mouthed the prayers. And then something cut through it all. A word. A thought. I don't remember if it was the Gospel reading or just the silence that finally got to me, but in the middle of Mass, one word bloomed in my chest like an old wound opening again.

Grace.

It wasn't gentle. It wasn't poetic. It was a punch. Grace. That was the word. Uninvited, unearned, and yet unmistakable. And immediately, my mind went back…not to a theology class or a scripture passage…but to a song. *Amazing Grace.* Not the whole thing. Just the opening. "Amazing Grace, how sweet the sound..." And I was no longer in the pew. I was back helping my dad plan my grandmother's funeral, years ago, standing beside my dad as we picked out songs. I'd suggested that one without thinking too hard about it. It just felt right. Sacred. But I didn't understand it then. Not really. I didn't understand grace. Not the way I do now.

Back then, grace was a word people threw around in church. A beautiful word, sure, but vague. Something for the pious. Something for priests and poets and people who didn't cuss under their breath during arguments with their wife. Something for people who hadn't knelt in a plywood hut in Afghanistan, begging God to make sense of the senseless. Something for the unbroken. I was far from that.

But in that Easter Mass, something shifted. Not a revelation. Not a vision. Just a crack in the wall I'd built around my soul. A whisper. *Write it.* Not because I had the answers. Not because I was healed. But because something in me had been seen. Exposed. And still…still, I felt loved. Still, I felt called. And I knew then, as strange as it felt to admit, that I was supposed to share that.

Not preach. Not teach. Just share.

Grace didn't come to me wrapped in certainty. It came with a memory of a hymn and the scent of incense. It came not when I was strong, but when I was standing silently, still broken, in the presence of a God who never left even when I had.

That's when I understood: I wasn't supposed to write about a finished product. I was supposed to write as one still being restored. Grace doesn't wait until you're polished. It shows up in the middle of the mess and says, *Even now, I'm here.*

And maybe, just maybe, you've felt that whisper too.

Part 2: I'm Still Unfinished

Let me say it plain: this isn't a "how I conquered my demons" story. It's not a polished redemption arc wrapped in a neat bow of faith. I didn't walk out of Afghanistan with the glow of a spiritual awakening. I didn't return from war to become a motivational speaker. And I'm not writing this book because I've arrived at some enlightened place where I now float above the pain of life. I'm writing it because I haven't. I'm writing it because I'm still in the middle of it.

Still unfinished…but a work *in progress.*

There are mornings I wake up and can't figure out why I feel that weight in my chest...like something's broken before the day even begins. I go through the routine. Shower. A Monster (not a coffee drinker). Kids. Work. But underneath it all is this low hum of tension. Like my soul is bracing for an impact it can't name. Some days it's manageable. Some days it's a full-body fatigue. And other days...it's the kind of quiet unraveling that no one sees but you feel down to your bones. That's the part no one tells you about survival. The part that lingers after the big moments have passed. The way trauma embeds itself not just in your memory, but in your calendar. In your habits. In your reactions.

There are scars on my marriage...ones I didn't always see being made. Not from anything headline-worthy but... From silence. From numbness. From being so locked inside my own pain that I didn't have the bandwidth to hold hers. I've never doubted my love for my wife. But there were months where I forgot how to show it. And there were years where she carried both of us when I didn't even realize I'd gone missing.

There are scars in my faith, too. Deep ones. For a long time, I didn't know how to talk to God not due to anger but from indifference. I didn't stop believing. But belief and connection are not the same thing. And belief without connection? That's spiritual starvation. That's knowing the Eucharist is there and choosing to stand outside the church because you're not sure you deserve to kneel.

And then there's the body...my body. The toll doesn't show in the obvious ways. No missing limbs. No visible injuries. But the nervous system remembers. The body keeps the score. I still startle too easily. Crowds still make my skin crawl. I've left meetings in high-level executive roles because the pressure cooker of conversation triggered a cold sweat and a desperate need for air. I've faked stomach bugs, phone calls, distractions...just to escape without tipping my hand.

So if you're looking for a tidy before-and-after story, you won't find it here. What you'll find is something messier. Truer. A story still unfolding.

You'll find Afghanistan...not as a place, but as a fracture in the timeline. The moment when things stopped making sense. When I realized there are children on this planet whose lives matter less to some simply because of where they were born. When I held dying men's hands and didn't have words, just pressure. When I saw people live who had no business surviving, and others die who were supposed to make it. And when I stopped pretending that faith was immune to doubt.

You'll find the story of Rwanda...years later...a place I traveled to expecting little and returning with pieces of my humanity stitched back together by the love and laughter of people who had every reason to hate and instead chose hope. You'll find my wife's patience...grace in yoga pants, kids, laundry, and silent prayers whispered from across the bed when I couldn't sleep.

You'll find July 4th. Not the fireworks, but the fear. My kids ooh'ing and ahh'ing, watching a fireworks show, and me...sweating, pacing, trying not to flinch with every boom. Trying to fake normal for them, while my mind played back the pop-pop-pop of a memory I couldn't mute. You'll find leadership roles I performed well in, while secretly wondering how long I could keep pretending I wasn't unraveling under the weight of my own chest.

But you'll also find this: I'm still here.

And maybe that's the beginning of grace. Not perfection. Not clarity. Not victory. But presence. Still standing. Still waking up. Still trying. Still loved...even when I don't feel lovable. Still married...even when I didn't know how to be a husband. Still fathering, even when I didn't feel like a man worth following. Still praying, in fits and starts, even when the prayers feel dry as dust.

Grace doesn't wait for you to get your act together. It doesn't demand a résumé of righteousness. It doesn't audit your performance before deciding whether you qualify. Grace shows up in the middle of the mess and stays. Not because you earned it. Not because you deserve it. But because that's what grace does.

I used to think grace was for the people in the choir...the ones who got it right. Now I know it's for the guy in the back row, arms crossed, heart numb, trying not to bolt for the door. It's for the soldier kneeling in blood and dirt, unsure whether he believes in God but still hoping someone hears his cry. It's for the father who screws up bedtime for the fifth night in a row and doesn't know how to apologize without crying. It's for the husband who keeps trying, even when love feels more like a choice than a feeling. It's for the man who stares at the mirror and doesn't recognize the face looking back...and for the one who still hopes that maybe, somehow, he can become whole again.

I don't know where you're reading this. I don't know what you've lived through. But if you're reading this wondering whether grace is still available to someone like you, I'll tell you the truth I've come to understand the hard way:

It is.

Not because you're ready. Not because you've healed. But because grace doesn't come to people who deserve it. It comes to the broken. The burdened. The barely hanging on. People like me. Maybe people like you.

I'm still unfinished. And that, somehow, is the point, as that is the very definition of Grace.

Part 3: The Power and Problem of Grace

Let me be honest about something most people don't say out loud in church: grace can be a problem. Not because it's weak. But because it's strong in all the wrong ways. Because it doesn't follow our logic. Because it offers healing before we've finished bleeding. Because it insists on loving us even when we're still doing the thing we swore we'd never do again.

And if I'm being even more honest...grace has frustrated me more than once.

I used to think grace was something polite. A kind word. A second chance. Something beautiful, soft, maybe even sentimental. The kind of thing you hear about in Sunday school or in a wedding homily...something embroidered on a throw pillow or printed on a coffee mug with a watercolor font. But that's not what I've known it to be.

Grace, when it actually hit my life, didn't whisper. It invaded. Not with thunder, but with this steady insistence that refused to leave me alone. It showed up when I didn't want it. It stayed when I tried to outrun it. It spoke when I tried to drown it out with noise, work, guilt, distraction. Grace is persistent. And sometimes, that makes it feel like an interruption rather than a gift.

Because here's the thing no one tells you: when grace starts working in your life, it usually doesn't make you feel better right away. It makes you aware. Aware of the stuff you've been carrying. Aware of how tightly you've clenched your jaw for years. Aware of the distance you've created between yourself and God, between yourself and your spouse, between yourself and the version of you that used to dream. Grace doesn't come in and wave a magic wand over your pain. It comes in and shines a light on it...and then waits with you while you decide whether to let it heal you.

For years, I thought grace was something I had to be worthy of. Something I could disqualify myself from. So I disqualified myself. Over and over again. Because when you've held the hand of a dying man and said nothing, when you've yelled at your kids because you're not actually angry at them but at something you still haven't named, when you've shut down emotionally in the middle of your marriage because it feels safer to be numb than to be known...how could grace still apply to someone like that?

I thought grace was a reward. Now I know it's a lifeline.

It's the moment I stood in the shower, unable to stop shaking, staring at the tiled wall like it held some secret I'd missed. It's the memory of walking into Mass and not feeling anything...no goosebumps, no holy sentiment...and staying anyway. Sitting anyway. Whispering anyway. It's the sound of my wife's voice, calm when I didn't deserve calm, choosing love when I gave her silence. It's my kids climbing onto my lap when I felt most unworthy of their affection, as if God used their small hands to remind me I was still theirs. Still a father. Still here.

And it's the song. *Amazing Grace.*

It doesn't matter how many times I hear it...something in me reacts. Sometimes I cry. Sometimes I just go still. Not always from sadness, but from recognition. That first line alone carries more theology than a thousand sermons: "Amazing Grace, how sweet the sound." Why is grace a sound? Because you can't always see it. You can't always define it. But sometimes you hear it. Sometimes you feel it resonate inside of you, like a tuning fork against your ribs. You hear it in the silence of your wife not walking away. You hear it in your child's laugh on a day you thought you were still broken. You hear it in your own breath...steady, alive, undeserved.

The problem of grace is that it refuses to play by our rules. We want karma. We want fairness. We want people to get what they deserve. Until we're the ones on the mat, gasping for air, and what we need isn't fairness...it's mercy.

Grace doesn't make the pain disappear. It just gives the pain purpose. It doesn't erase the trauma. It teaches you how to carry it differently. And it doesn't always come with a feeling. Sometimes it comes with nothing but the ability to make it through another hour without collapsing. And somehow, that's enough.

I used to think grace was a moment. I don't anymore.

Grace is a lens.

Once it enters your life...not just as an idea but as an encounter...it changes how you see everything. You start looking at your wounds differently. Not with pride. Not with pity. But with clarity. That scar on your soul? You stop hiding it. You stop trying to sand it off. You start asking, *What if this is the mark of being carried through something I shouldn't have survived?*

You start looking at other people differently too. That guy yelling at the barista? Maybe he's on the edge of something you can't see. That coworker who flakes on meetings? Maybe she's surviving something every day. Grace doesn't just soften you. It gives you eyes. It doesn't make you blind to sin or weakness...but it lets you see through it. Past it. Into the ache beneath the anger. Into the story beneath the failure.

But I'll warn you: grace is not safe. It will ruin your self-righteousness. It will wreck your illusions. It will strip away every lie you use to prop yourself up...and then, when you're standing there exposed, it will wrap you in something stronger than shame. It will say, *Even now. Even here. I'm still with you.*

The real power of grace is not in what it gives. It's in what it reveals.

It reveals who you are without it. And who you are with it.

Without grace, I am a man who can't forgive himself. With it, I'm a man learning to parent, to lead, to love, not because I've earned redemption but because I've been given it freely. Without grace, I'm a veteran who's defined by what I've seen. With it, I'm a witness who can hold space for others to name what they've seen too. Without grace, I'm just another broken man pretending to be fine. With it...I'm still broken. But I'm honest. And I'm still moving.

Grace didn't fix me. It found me.

It didn't shout. It stayed.

It didn't explain. It held.

And if I have one prayer for this book, it's this: that you'll start to see it too.

Not just in mountaintop moments, not just in church pews. But in traffic. In laundry. In the way someone hugs you without needing a reason. In the nights you don't sleep, but still wake up and try again. In the days you can't pray, but you still whisper His name.

That's where grace lives. Not in perfection. In presence.

And it's closer than you think.

Part 4: Why This Book Exists

I didn't sit down to write a book. I sat down because something in me wouldn't shut up.

It wasn't ambition. It wasn't some bucket-list dream. It wasn't a pitch or a plan. It was Easter morning. And something cracked open inside me.

Not a loud crack. A quiet one. Like a hairline fracture you don't notice until you try to stand on it. One word split the silence of my internal numbness, and it was enough to rearrange me: *Grace.*

I didn't fully understand what was happening that day in the pew. Still don't. But I knew this much...there was something I was being asked to do. Not for applause. Not for publishing. Not even for catharsis. For obedience. For witness.

That's what this book is.

Not a sermon.

Not a memoir.

Not a message from someone who has it figured out.

It's a dispatch from the middle of the war. From a man still limping. From a husband who's caused harm and is still trying to rebuild trust. From a father who's learning, slowly, how to be emotionally present with kids who never asked for a version of dad who jumps at loud sounds or flinches at crowds. From a veteran who can still see the inside of a trauma tent with disturbing clarity. From a believer who sometimes struggles to feel God, but can't seem to deny His fingerprints.

I started writing this because I had to.

Because there were too many days where I could feel something important slipping...memories, meaning, even faith...and I knew that if I didn't capture it now, I might never retrieve it. So I wrote. Not with confidence. Not with eloquence. But with the kind of trembling urgency that comes when your soul taps you on the shoulder and says, *You're not done. Tell the truth.*

And that's really all this book is...truth. Or at least, the most honest truth I can tell at this point in my life.

I'm not offering advice. I'm not offering closure. I'm not offering answers that sound neat and tidy and printable on laminated bookmarks. I'm offering what I know: that grace is real, that it's relentless, and that it reaches into places you didn't even think deserved rescue.

This isn't a story about transformation in the way we usually talk about it. I'm not the "before and after" guy. I'm the "during" guy. I'm the "still in process" guy. The "some days I trust God and some days I don't know how to pray" guy. The "sometimes I feel joy and sometimes I feel numb" guy.

So if you came here expecting a formula, I'll disappoint you quickly.

But if you're looking for a companion...someone to sit beside you in the fog and not try to rush you out of it...maybe I can offer that. Maybe that's what this book can be.

I don't know what you need from these pages. I don't know your wounds, your past, or the weight you're carrying. I don't know where your marriage is, or what keeps you up at night, or what made you stop talking to God.

But I know you're still here. Still reading. And that counts for something.

That tells me there's a flicker still alive in you.

That flicker matters.

Because here's the thing about grace: it doesn't need a bonfire to start working. It'll start with a flicker. A breath. A whispered prayer. A moment of honesty when everything in you wants to shut down.

You don't need to be holy to receive grace.

You don't need to be emotionally stable. Or spiritually strong. Or religiously consistent.

You don't even need to be "ready."

You just need to be real.

I think a lot about the people who might pick up this book. Not the ones looking to be inspired. But the ones looking to not feel alone. The ones who feel like they're on the fence...not against God, but not exactly walking with Him either. The ones who're doing their best but feel like their best isn't enough. The ones who stood in church one day and wondered if they belonged there. The ones who've loved deeply and hurt deeply. The ones who still carry names, faces, moments, guilt, prayers they haven't said in years.

This book is for you.

For the version of me that sat in Afghanistan trying to reconcile a loving God with what I saw done to women and children.

For the man who came home from war but couldn't come home to himself.

For the husband who struggles to say the things he feels.

For the father who panics when the fireworks start.

For the leader who sits at the head of a table but feels like he's hiding something cracked beneath his pressed shirt.

For the Christian who can quote Scripture but hasn't felt God in months.

And for the person who doesn't even know why they picked up this book...but something in the title pulled at them. *Amazing Grace.* Not as a song. Not as a sentiment. But as a dare: What if this is still possible for you?

That's what I'm hoping for. Not resolution. Recognition.

I want you to recognize grace when it whispers your name.

I want you to see it in the small moments that hold you together when you thought you might fall apart.

I want you to hear it in the silence after a long cry, when nothing has changed except that you're still breathing.

I want you to begin seeing again...not with perfect vision, but with awakened eyes.

Because the only thing worse than being blind… is being numb.

This book is my invitation to you: not to get it all together. But to let grace meet you where you are.

To see again.

Not just what happened.

But who held you.

Not just what broke.

But what still breathes.

Not just what you lost.

But what grace kept alive in you, even when you forgot it was there.

Part 5: Scripture and the Scar

There's a scar on my left thumb...just below the joint. It's not big, maybe an inch at most, faded to a pale white now. I got it during a training exercise, years before deployment. We were running trauma drills on a mock casualty...plastic mannequin, fake blood, controlled chaos. Somewhere in the scramble to open a chest seal packet, my hand slipped, and the knife edge caught me. Just a clean slice. Nothing dramatic.

But the scar stayed.

It healed, of course. No stitches. Just time, pressure, and antiseptic. But even now, all these years later, I'll catch sight of it on a steering wheel, or holding a fork, or folding laundry...and I'll remember.

Not the pain, exactly.

The context.

The moment.

And the fact that healing leaves a mark.

It makes me think of the verse...**John 9:25.** You probably know it. Even if you've never memorized Scripture, this one's found its way into enough songs and sermons to be familiar even if you never realized it comes from scripture: *"I was blind, and now I see."*

It's the testimony of a man healed by Jesus...once a beggar, now standing in front of the religious elite, grilled about a miracle they didn't like. He doesn't give a theological treatise. He doesn't explain Christ's divinity. He doesn't even try to answer their suspicions. He just gives them his scar story.

"I was blind. Now I see."

That's it.

He lets his scar speak.

That's the kind of testimony I've come to understand. Not polished. Not rehearsed. Just undeniable. And that's what I'm trying to offer here...not an argument for grace, but evidence of it. Not through credentials. Through scars.

Because I don't believe we were meant to follow Jesus out of persuasion. I believe we were meant to follow Him out of encounter. And if you've encountered grace, even once, you know: it doesn't leave you the same.

You walk away seeing differently.

Sometimes that's a blessing. Sometimes it's a burden.

I see my wife differently now. I used to see her as a partner in a shared mission. A teammate. Now I see her as something holier...someone who absorbed more than I ever gave her credit for. Who caught the shrapnel of my silence and kept showing up anyway. Who prayed in the kitchen, while I worked on some project in the garage, trying to make sense of a war I never finished leaving.

I see my kids differently. Not as projects or responsibilities. As gifts. Living reminders that grace is often loud, messy, and giggling. I used to panic about whether I was failing them. Now I realize...grace meets them too. Through my presence. Through my apologies. Through the simple act of holding them, even when I feel unworthy.

I see God differently. Not as a concept. Not as a judge. Not even as a healer. As a witness.

I believe God was there when I stood over the body of a man we couldn't save.

I believe He was there when I sat on the edge of my bed at 3am, debating whether to tell my wife how bad the panic attacks had gotten.

I believe He was there when I whispered prayers I didn't believe in...just in case someone was still listening.

And I believe He's here now. In this moment. With you. Wherever you're sitting. Reading this. Holding your own scar story.

There's another verse that stays close to me...**2 Corinthians 12:9**. Paul says he begged God to take away his affliction, his "thorn." Whatever it was, it was enough to make him plead for relief. And God's answer?

"My grace is sufficient for you, for my power is made perfect in weakness."

I used to read that verse like it was supposed to comfort me.

Now I read it like it's supposed to center me.

God didn't remove Paul's thorn. He revealed Himself in it.

That changes everything.

It means the goal isn't to get clean. The goal is to let grace be visible...right where the pain still lingers.

It means your wounds don't have to vanish to make you usable.

It means your numbness doesn't disqualify you.

It means your unanswered questions aren't obstacles. They're altars.

And it means that the scar you keep trying to hide might be the place where grace wants to speak.

So when people ask me what this book is about, I could quote Scripture. I could say it's about Romans 5:8..."While we were still sinners, Christ died for us." I could say it's about the love that comes before the clean-up. I could say it's about healing. Hope. Even redemption.

But the truth?

This book is about scars.

The ones you see. The ones you don't. The ones you carry in silence.

And the fact that, by grace, they aren't just remnants of pain. They're witnesses to mercy.

Grace doesn't erase what happened. It reframes it.

It doesn't change the past. It changes your posture toward it.

It doesn't make your story shiny. It makes it sacred.

So let the scar stay. Let it remind you. Not of the wound...but of the One who stayed with you through it.

This is not a book from someone who has arrived. This is a book from someone who was blind...and by some miracle of grace, is starting to see again.

Not perfectly.

Not completely.

But clearly enough to say:

Grace was there.
Grace is still here.
And it's not done with us yet.

Before you move on, pause with this:

Reflection Hook for the Reader

What's the moment that first made you wonder if grace might be real?

Was it quiet or loud? Was it full of light, or just barely enough to see by? Maybe it wasn't dramatic at all...maybe it was just a moment you survived when you thought you wouldn't. Maybe it was someone who stayed. A whisper that told you not to quit. A prayer you didn't expect to work, but did.

And second:

What scars in your life still need new meaning?

Not to be erased. Not to be justified. Just to be seen...again, through different eyes. What if the scar itself is not the end of the story, but the start of a witness?

Write it down. Or just sit with it. This isn't about fixing anything yet.

It's about naming what grace might still want to touch.

Part 1: The Decision Nobody Understood

It's strange how grace can sound like a dare.

Not the kind that thrills you...but the kind that wakes you at 3am and sits on your chest like a question you can't shake.

That's what it felt like.

I was 35. Married. Father of two. I had a master's degree. An executive-level career in real estate development. A salary. Health insurance. A family that needed me. And yet, there it was...that quiet, irrational, insistent call.

Go.

That's all it was. No thunder. No clarity. Just this whisper lodged in my chest that wouldn't leave me alone.

I didn't feel brave. I wasn't looking for glory. I wasn't chasing anything, really. If anything, I was trying to outrun the nagging sense that I had been given much...and hadn't yet offered enough in return.

I still remember sitting at the kitchen table when I told Cathy.

I'd been turning it over in my mind for months. Running the numbers. Running from the implications. Asking the same question in circles: *Is this madness...or obedience?*

And finally, it spilled out.

"I think I'm supposed to enlist."

I said it like a confession. Not a declaration. Not a request. Just something I had to name before it consumed me.

She didn't speak right away.

She didn't cry, either.

She just looked at me for a long time. Studying my face. Measuring the weight of what I'd said. She knew me well enough to recognize that this wasn't a whim. But even still, I could see the heartbreak settle behind her eyes like a slow tide.

"Why?" she asked.

It wasn't judgment. It was bewilderment.

And truthfully? I didn't have a good answer. Not one that would pass a financial advisor's audit. Not one that would make sense at a dinner party. Not one that would comfort a wife who was already holding our household together.

I said something about purpose. About the feeling I couldn't shake. About the words of Thomas Paine I'd always admired: *"If there must be trouble, let it be in my day, that my child may have peace."*

I don't know if that helped. I doubt it did.

But she nodded.

Not because she understood.

Because she loved me.

And I've come to see that nod...not as consent, but as courage. A kind of grace I didn't deserve and certainly hadn't earned.

I expected people not to get it. And they didn't.

"Are you serious?" a friend said. "Man, you're old enough to be their dad."

"You've got a job people would kill for. Why throw that away now?"

"You're going to be a private? At your age?"

One colleague didn't even try to hide his laugh. "Midlife crisis much?"

I smiled. I let the comments roll. But what none of them saw was how many nights I had lain awake trying to talk myself out of it. Trying to reason with that stubborn ache in my chest. And how every time I tried to walk away from the idea, it followed me like a shadow.

It didn't feel rational…and by most "normal" measures, it wasn't rational.

But it felt right.

I wasn't chasing adventure. I was obeying a whisper.

That whisper wasn't loud. It wasn't dramatic. It didn't come with angelic trumpets or burning bushes. It came through silence. Through an unshakeable conviction. Through the deep, haunting question that kept coming back: *What if you don't?*

That's what calling feels like sometimes...not a passion, but a burden. Not a path that lights up in gold, but a road you step onto in the dark, simply because you can't not walk it.

I've never once felt heroic about the decision.

In fact, there was more doubt than resolve in those early days. More nausea than nobility.

Because once the enlistment papers were signed, the real consequences started to unfold.

I had to tell the kids.

We had to prepare for months of training. For the unknown.

And that's when the gravity hit: obedience isn't the end of wrestling. It's the beginning.

Later, after receiving deployment orders, there were nights Cathy would sit on the couch, hands folded in her lap, looking at me like a stranger. Not cold. Just distant. Like she was already preparing for the part of me that would be gone. Preparing to parent alone. Preparing to explain my absence to our children. Preparing for a reality she never asked for but was about to inherit.

It would've been easier if she had yelled. Or accused. Or stormed out.

But she didn't.

She just stayed.

That's how I first began to recognize what grace looks like in real life. Not in stained glass, but in the silence between husband and wife when the road ahead is terrifying and love still holds its ground.

There's a part of me that still wonders what exactly was calling me. Was it God? Was it guilt? Was it something buried in my past or some unmet need to prove something?

Maybe a mix of all of it.

But what I know is this: it wasn't ego. It wasn't a death wish. It wasn't a crisis.

It was a calling.

A quiet, disorienting call that disrupted everything...but didn't destroy me.

And that, too, was grace.

Not the comforting kind.

The shaking kind.

The kind that knocks over your perfectly stacked plans and says, *Now I can begin something holy.*

Part 2: Obedience Isn't Clarity. It's Cost.

There's this unspoken myth floating around in Christian circles...the idea that if God calls you to something, He'll pave the road with clarity and confirmation. That obedience will be rewarded with peace. That the right decision will "feel right," and everything will fall into place.

Let me tell you: that's not how it went.

Obedience didn't feel like peace. It felt like jumping off a ledge blindfolded, hoping I'd land somewhere close to faith.

The moment I left for boot camp, the fantasy ended. The disruption began.

Suddenly, everything was a negotiation...between duty and guilt, conviction and consequence.

There was the money. Let's just start there. I went from a six-figure career to a recruit's paycheck. Not a demotion...an implosion. We cut expenses, reprioritized everything, and carried the weight of "just get through this year" like a mantra we chanted in private.

But the financial strain was only the surface cost.

Emotionally, the fallout was slower, but deeper.

The weeks leading up to deployment, I could feel Cathy slipping behind her eyes. Still present. Still functioning. But more reserved. Like someone walking around their home before a storm, moving things inside, bracing for impact.

We never had explosive fights during that season. That might've been easier, honestly. Fights bring release. We just slowly stopped talking about anything deeper than logistics. School schedules. Groceries. Laundry. It was like we were standing on either side of a cracked bridge, both of us pretending we could still meet in the middle, when really...we were just waving from opposite banks.

One night, she finally said it.

"I know why you're doing this. And I'm trying to support it. But it feels like you chose this over us."

I didn't have an answer. Because in a way, she was right. I had chosen something...some blurry, God-whispered conviction...over the stability of our family. Over her security. Over our shared timeline.

And this is where it gets messy: I didn't feel righteous about it. I didn't feel triumphant. I felt torn. Gutted. Like a man who'd lit a match in a dry room and now had to watch what it scorched.

You don't get to follow a calling without it costing someone else something too…in some ways I now think it costs others more than the one following the call.

And that's the part we don't talk about enough. We celebrate obedience. But we rarely talk about what it extracts.

When Abraham left everything, it wasn't just his story. Sarah had to pack her life too.

When Mary said, "Let it be done to me," her world...and her reputation...was undone.

We love the poetry of obedience. But we flinch at the price tag.

For Cathy, the cost wasn't in the goodbye at the airport. It was in the thirteen months of doing life solo. In the nights when our son was sick and she had no one to tag in. In the early mornings when the kids actually slept in and the silence in our bedroom was louder than any explosion I heard overseas.

For me, the cost came in waves.

It came during basic training, when I realized I was twice the age of some of the guys in my unit and still had to act like we were the same. It came when I watched Cathy's eyes glass over on video calls, both of us pretending that this was fine, that we were fine, that love was enough to fill the widening gap between us.

And it came in the questions I didn't have answers for.

Was this really God's will?

Was I just chasing a feeling from God, or myself?

Was grace supposed to feel this heavy?

I wanted to believe that if God had really called me, He would show up in clear, unmistakable ways. That I'd feel buoyed by His presence. That I'd come home to a marriage that had somehow grown stronger in my absence. That I'd experience alignment.

Instead, what I felt was tension.

Disorientation.

And more silence than I knew what to do with.

This wasn't grace as comfort. This was grace as confrontation.

Obedience doesn't guarantee relief. Sometimes it guarantees rupture.

And I began to realize: maybe I had misunderstood the point. Maybe grace isn't there to make things easier. Maybe it's there to make them *truer.*

To reveal what's fragile.

To draw out what's hidden.

To burn away what can't survive the fire.

I'd grown up believing in God's faithfulness. But it wasn't until this season that I had to wrestle with what that actually meant. Faithfulness doesn't always mean feeling held. Sometimes it means walking in the dark with no map, wondering where God is, and trying to believe that He's still leading.

It's **Hebrews 11:8** in real life: *"By faith Abraham obeyed... not knowing where he was going."*

Not knowing. Still going.

That was me.

And maybe that's you.

Maybe you've said yes to something that made no sense. Maybe you're knee-deep in the fallout. Maybe grace hasn't delivered the clarity you hoped for.

Let me tell you something that might not be comforting but is absolutely true: that doesn't mean you heard wrong.

Sometimes the only sign that you're following God is that things get harder.

Not because He wants you to suffer.

But because grace isn't always a balm.

Sometimes it's a blade.

It cuts away illusions.

It reveals the idols you didn't know you were still holding...comfort, control, certainty.

And it asks, *Will you still follow Me, even now? Even here?*

I didn't know it at the time, but the pain we were in...Cathy and I...was part of the fire grace was allowing us to walk through. Not to destroy us. To deepen us. Not to punish us. To purify something we'd let rust through routine.

But I wouldn't have said that then.

Back then, all I knew was: I'd said yes.

And grace hadn't made it easier.

But I wasn't turning back.

Part 3: What Grace Actually Did

There's a strange kind of grace that doesn't stop the storm. It just anchors you while it rages.

For most of that first year, I didn't see it.

I looked for grace in the wrong places...in outcomes, in clarity, in confirmation. I kept waiting for some divine "aha moment," where everything would click and I'd say, *Ah, now I see what God was doing.* But no such moment came. Not then.

Instead, grace slipped in through the cracks. Subtle. Steady. Unspectacular, except in hindsight.

It came in the shape of a woman folding laundry alone.

Cathy never once tried to manipulate me with guilt during that season. She had every reason to. She could've reminded me daily of what I was missing: birthday parties, dance recitals, the ache of a bed half-empty, the decisions she was forced to make solo.

But she didn't weaponize the weight. She carried it.

And she did it with a quiet, weary dignity I didn't fully recognize until much later.

That's the thing about real grace...it rarely raises its voice. It doesn't draw attention to itself. It just shows up. Stays. Endures.

There was this one moment, shortly before I left for basic training. We were sitting in the living room, surrounded by the few bags I had packed. I was stressed, distracted, trying to mentally prepare for the separation.

Cathy was sitting across from me, legs curled under her, nursing a mug of cold tea she hadn't touched in an hour.

We weren't talking much.

Finally, she broke the silence.

"I need you to know something," she said. "I don't understand this. I don't even like it. But I believe that you believe, you're supposed to do it. So I'm going to support you on it. I just need you to come back the man I married."

She didn't cry. She didn't ask for anything more.

She was giving me her permission...not because I asked for it, but because she knew I needed it even if I didn't.

That moment became a compass I would come back to again and again.

Because when the days were long, and the training broke me down, and I felt like a middle-aged imposter trying to keep up with 18-year-olds who'd never had a mortgage, men who I had to teach to address and mail a letter, I remembered her voice. Not angry. Not resigned. Just faithful.

That's what grace did.

It didn't pave the way. It stood in the gap.

It didn't eliminate the cost. It refused to let the cost define the story.

Even in the middle of basic training...when the exhaustion was more mental than physical, and I found myself wondering what I had done...I started to see it again. Not in blinding flashes. But in moments I almost missed.

One afternoon, after a brutal ruck march, one of the younger guys in our platoon wanted to give up and drop out. I tighten my pack and was at his side before anyone else moved, age and experience kicking in without hesitation. Kneeling next to him, I took his rifle, to carry and told him not to give the drill sergeants the satisfaction…that if my "old ass" could do it, he could to, I heard the drill sergeant mutter something to another NCO behind me.

"Old man knows what he's doing."

It wasn't a compliment exactly. But it stuck with me.

I wasn't there to prove I could be twenty again. I was there because I had something different to offer. And in that moment, grace showed up through clarity of purpose. Not ego. Not applause. Just usefulness…a usefulness born of age and experience.

A few nights later, I found myself writing a letter to Cathy. Nothing profound. Just a thank-you. Not for the support. But for the sacrifice.

I told her I didn't know how she was doing it...managing the house, the bills, the loneliness. I told her I wasn't even sure I was making the right call anymore. But I was grateful for her still being there.

I didn't expect her to reply right away. Mail was slow. Schedules were unpredictable.

But a week later, I opened a reply that changed me.

She didn't analyze. She didn't soothe. She just wrote this:

"I don't know if this is the right path either. But I know God doesn't waste the ones we walk in faith. I miss you. I believe in you. We'll be waiting."

That's when I knew: grace wasn't going to remove the ache. It was going to make the ache bearable.

That letter sat tucked in my bible that I carried for weeks.

I carried it through drills. Through inspections. Through days where my joints ached and my lungs burned and I felt like a ghost in someone else's story.

And every time I touched that envelope in my uniform, I remembered: I wasn't alone.

God hadn't removed the weight...but He'd made sure I had a reason to keep walking with it.

So often, we miss the work of grace because it doesn't come how we imagined.

We picture grace as rescue.

But sometimes, more often than not, grace is just *presence.*

It's the breath to finish the sentence when you feel like collapsing.

It's the letter you didn't know you needed.

It's the woman who keeps showing up, even when she could be packing her bags.

It's God not offering answers...but offering nearness.

When I look back on that season now, I still wouldn't call it peaceful.

But I would call it sacred.

Because I know grace was there. Not erasing the chaos. But holding it with me.

And maybe that's the most powerful kind of grace...the kind that doesn't remove the storm.

The kind that climbs in the boat with you, holds your hand, and says, *We're not done yet.*

Part 4: Grace and Calling Are Often Confused

I wish I could tell you I knew exactly why I enlisted.

I wish I had a crisp mission statement, a journal entry that mapped it all out. I wish I could point to one defining reason...the kind that silences doubters and satisfies editors.

But the truth is murkier.

At 35, with a family and a life already in motion, I stood on the edge of a choice that didn't make sense to anyone...including me. And I made it anyway.

Because something in me couldn't not.

There's a phrase that's haunted me in the best way: *"God doesn't always speak in complete sentences."*

That's what this was. Not a paragraph. Not even a full line. Just a fragment of a whisper, lodged somewhere between calling and compulsion. Something unshakable. Something I couldn't logic away.

I didn't feel peace. I felt pulled.

And that's the tension no one prepares you for...that calling doesn't always arrive with clarity. Sometimes it comes cloaked in restlessness. Sometimes it's wrapped in silence. Sometimes the only evidence you have is that *not* obeying would feel like a kind of death.

I still remember a conversation with an old friend, a fellow believer, someone who loved me and meant well. We were having lunch a few weeks after I enlisted.

He leaned back in his chair and said, "I just don't get it, man. You've built a life. You've got people depending on you. Are you sure this isn't just... unresolved stuff?"

He said it kindly. But I felt the sting.

Unresolved stuff.

Maybe it was. Maybe part of me needed to prove I still had edge. Maybe part of me hadn't made peace with the world's brokenness and needed to enter it more directly. Maybe I was trying to show God...and myself...that I could still be useful.

But calling doesn't always arise from purity.

Sometimes it's a mix of faith and fire and wound and wonder.

And I've learned that grace isn't scared of our mixed motives. It works with what's true.

If you wait to be totally sure before you step forward, you'll never move.

I used to think that discerning your calling meant achieving certainty. Now I think it means saying yes to God *before* certainty.

It's **Luke 1:38**...Mary saying, *"Let it be done to me according to your word."* No plan. No map. Just surrender.

It's **Matthew 26:39**...Jesus, sweating blood, praying, *"Not as I will, but as you will."*

It's the decision to walk into mystery.

I didn't know what God was doing when I signed those enlistment papers.

I still don't fully know.

But looking back now, I see fingerprints.

I see the way Cathy's strength grew roots I didn't know she had.

I see the way our kids watched their dad choose service over safety...and the questions that sparked.

I see how my training would later save lives I hadn't yet met. How it would teach me to think calmly in chaos. How it would prepare me for decisions I wouldn't want to make...but would need to.

I see how that year burned off ego and exposed weakness...not to shame me, but to prepare me for grace.

And maybe that's the deeper purpose of calling...not achievement, but excavation.

Maybe God calls us not to build a résumé, but to unearth who we really are.

Maybe grace uses calling not to make us impressive...but to make us *whole.*

It took me years to admit that I still don't know the full "why" behind my enlistment. But I no longer need to.

Because grace doesn't always explain itself.

It invites.

It disrupts.

It provokes.

It stirs the waters of comfort and calls you to step out anyway...not because the outcome is guaranteed, but because something holy waits in the walking.

And here's what I've come to believe: if grace is truly present, it will grow fruit in you even when you don't understand the soil.

You don't need to decode the whole story right now.

You just need to keep walking, eyes open, hands open, heart willing.

If the road you're on feels uncertain, if the "why" is still blurry, if you're obeying a voice you can't explain to anyone else...you're not off track.

You might be right in the middle of grace.

Part 5: When Grace Doesn't Explain Itself – Grace in the Fog

If you're looking for a scar to show where this chapter of my life ended, you won't find one.

There's no dramatic exit wound. No physical marker. What changed wasn't visible.

But it was there.

The scar lived under the surface...an ache of having obeyed something sacred without fully understanding it. And sometimes, the deepest scars are those that form where no one else can see.

When I look at Scripture now, I notice something I never used to see: the best stories never begin with full understanding. They begin with obedience *into the fog.*

Hebrews 11:8 says it outright: *"By faith Abraham obeyed when he was called to go out to a place that he was to receive as an inheritance. And he went out, not knowing where he was going."*

That line used to frustrate me.

"Not knowing where he was going"? How is that a plan?

But the more life I live, the more that verse sounds like a mirror.

I didn't know where I was going either.

I just knew I had to go.

I had to trust that grace didn't require me to see the full path...only to take the next step.

It's an unsettling way to walk. Because it demands that you *keep walking* even when you don't feel God's hand on your back. It means you say "yes" not because of certainty...but because *you remember the whisper* that started all of it.

I don't know what Abraham's tent looked like on that first night out. But I imagine it was small. Sparse. Wind flapping at the edges. Maybe he lay there wondering if he had lost his mind. Wondering what he'd just dragged his family into. Maybe Sarah sat beside him, silent like Cathy was in our living room, staring into an unknown future, wondering what kind of God leads people into this kind of uncertainty.

And yet...they kept walking.

And God kept showing up.

Not with blueprints. But with presence.

I've come to realize something: *The fog doesn't mean you're lost. It means you're walking by faith.*

Faith doesn't mean confidence.

Faith means movement in the absence of clarity.

Obedience means saying yes to God when the map is still blank and the destination is unspoken.

And grace...real grace...doesn't promise ease.

It promises presence.

The call I followed at 35 didn't make my life easier. It made it harder, in some ways. It forced me to wrestle with my identity, my marriage, my masculinity, my theology, my weakness. But it also made my life *truer.*

And I'd rather live a true life in fog than a false one in comfort.

That's the scar I carry now. Not of injury...but of awakening.

The scar of having walked into something holy without knowing how it would end.

The scar of choosing grace when it didn't look like blessing.

The scar of obeying a whisper instead of a command.

And maybe that's the most honest theology I can offer: that God is still trustworthy in the fog.

You don't need the full explanation. You don't need to understand how it ends.

You just need to know the One who called you is still calling.

Not because you're strong.

But because He is.

Not because you have the answers.

But because grace is willing to walk with you while you don't.

Reflection Hook for the Reader

Before you turn the page, take a moment with this:

What's the decision you made that didn't make sense...but you had to make it?

Not because it was strategic. Not because it looked good on paper. But because your soul knew it was necessary.

Where have you obeyed without understanding...and only later glimpsed grace?

Think back. What started messy but ended holy? What pain did you walk through that turned out to be a kind of preparation?

What might God be asking you to walk into now, even if it costs?

Where is the whisper calling you? What fog are you standing in? What obedience still scares you?

Write it down.

Name it.

Not to solve it.

Just to recognize that grace might be closer than you think.

Chapter 3: Afghanistan – The Year That Took Something

Part 1: Leaving Home

I've tried to remember what I did that morning.

Everything was already packed as we'd been in pre-mobilization training for a couple of months at this point already..

But what stands out now isn't what I did.

It's what Cathy didn't say.

She stood in the hallway, arms crossed, not angry, just… bracing. There was nothing left to talk about. No arguments. No last-minute bargains. We'd already had those. This was just the moment you pretend is normal, even when everything in you is screaming that it isn't.

Our kids were still asleep.

I turned to Cathy. She didn't smile. She didn't fall apart either. She just gave me a look that said everything. *Come back different...but come back.*

I stepped outside and glanced back at the house.

It looked so ordinary.

Brick facade. White trim. A tricycle half-tipped in the driveway. Curtains slightly parted. The smell of wet grass, morning dew, and the faint burn of summer rising from the street.

Would it all still be here when I got back?

Not the structure. The soul of it. The "us" of it.

No one tells you how hard it is to walk away from the life you love...not because you're running from it, but because you're trying to protect something deeper than words.

And yet, every step toward that airport felt like I was leaving something behind I couldn't carry with me.

Not physically.

Spiritually.

There's no ceremonial moment at the gate. No flags waving. No dramatic music. Just rows of men and women in uniform looking down at their phones, swiping through the faces they're about to leave. Flights get delayed. People yawn. You stare out the window and try to imagine the terrain that will soon be your normal.

There's a loneliness to it. A quiet ache. Not of fear...at least not in the way people imagine. It's heavier than that. It's grief before death. Anticipatory mourning for a version of you that won't survive the year.

The plane lifted off before sunrise. I stared out the window at the glow beginning to rise behind the city. Somewhere in that light were my wife, my kids, my bed, my ordinary rituals. Dinner together, VeggieTales cartoons, Toothpaste spit in the sink.

Gone in a blink.

And here I was...hurtling toward the unknown, full of questions, strapped to duty, with no real idea of what would be waiting when the wheels touched down in another world.

In my pocket, I carried a small copy of the New Testament, the same copy my father had carried in Vietnam over 40 years earlier.

The words that Cathy had spoken kept playing over and over in my mind.

"Don't come home just to survive. Come home more whole than you left. We'll still be here."

I closed my eyes. Breathed it in. Let the ache settle somewhere between courage and doubt.

She believed something for me that I hadn't yet found the words to believe myself.

And that's how grace started that year...not as comfort.

As presence.

As a woman's quiet strength holding space for something sacred I hadn't yet lived through.

I didn't feel ready.

But I was already gone.

And grace was already waiting in the middle of it all.

Part 2: The Fog of Daily Survival

No one warns you that war is mostly boredom.

Not boredom in the sense of nothing happening...but in the sense that the same things happen, over and over, until they stop feeling real. Until you stop feeling much at all.

I arrived in Afghanistan assigned to a Provincial Reconstruction Team...PRT, they called it. But "reconstruction" was a polite word. We did everything: escorting civil affairs officers to fragile meetings, guarding engineers as they surveyed damaged infrastructure, securing remote medical clinics that might as well have been built from cardboard.

My job was twofold: combat medic and security force. That meant I carried the tools to patch a man up, and the weapon to make sure we didn't need to. I learned quickly that the line between the two was thinner than I'd ever imagined.

Days blurred together.

Wake. Gear up. Patrol. Secure. Wait. Eat. Patrol again. Return. Decompress. Sleep...badly. Repeat.

There was no arc. No rising action. Just a loop.

The sun came up angry every morning, throwing heat across everything before 9 a.m…and later bitter cold. The dust was constant. It got inside your nose, your boots, your food. Your thoughts.

Generators hummed at night like a slow, anxious heartbeat. Helicopters landed and took off in an almost constant rhythm. There were always dogs barking in the distance...feral, desperate, persistent.

I remember the smell of diesel in the morning. Nitrile gloves powdered with talc. The sound of velcro ripping open at the worst times. The slick texture of sweat behind my knees during convoys. The uncomfortable intimacy of silence between teammates who had all seen too much and learned to say too little.

One morning, I found a piece of Afghan flatbread in my kit...left over from a goodwill stop we had made the day before. I ate it slowly, almost reverently. It was cold and slightly burned. But it tasted like something real. Like a reminder of the world outside our armored cocoon. I held it longer than I needed to. That was how rare softness became.

There were moments that stuck, but not for their violence. I thankfully saw little violence. I instead saw too much of the aftermath.

For their quiet weight.

Once, we treated a child who'd was badly injured. I don't remember how he was hurt. He wasn't our mission. But we stopped anyway. I remember lifting him into the back of the ambulance the locals had brought. His body limp, bleeding, barely crying. I didn't feel much. Just efficient.

Later that night, I stared at my hands. They still smelled like iodine.

And I realized I hadn't prayed once.

Not for him. Not for me.

Not out of anger. Just… numbness.

I wasn't surprised. That's what the fog does. It doesn't shout. It erases. Slowly. Repetitively. Until you wake up one day and don't remember what you used to feel like.

I had stopped calling home as much. I told Cathy I was just tired. That the connection was spotty. But the truth was harder: I didn't know what to say. What do you say when your soul feels beige? When the most honest thing you could admit is, *I'm still here. But I'm not sure how much longer I will be...at least not in the way you remember me.*

Sometimes I would reread her letters just to feel something. But even those began to fade, not in meaning, but *in my ability to access the emotion behind them.* Like they were written in a language I used to know.

That's the slow spiritual erosion no one trains you for.

You don't break all at once.

You wear down.

You thin out.

You become less of a person and more of a function. A shape in a uniform. A task in a rotation.

I remember lying in my bunk one night, watching a small moth circle the light above my head. Where did it come from? How had it survived here? It flew in a tight, frantic loop for nearly ten minutes. Then it landed, still.

I stared at it.

And all I could think was: *That's how I feel.*

Battered. Chasing something, not knowing why. Then still...not from peace, but from exhaustion.

Even Scripture felt distant.

I had my father's copy of the New Testament with me. I opened it occasionally, not for revelation, but out of…almost curiosity. I wondered if my dad had felt the same way, or worse. I know that what he saw in Vietnam made my experiences pale in comparison. Some days I just ran my thumb along the edges of the pages. I didn't read it. I just wanted to feel something holy.

But holiness was hard to touch in that place.

Not because God wasn't there. But because I was so far away from myself.

Some nights I would close my eyes and try to remember my son's laugh or my daughter's quiet cooing of a newborn.

And I couldn't.

I could picture them. But the sound was gone.

That was the moment I realized: something was being lost while I was there. No, something was being taken.

Not all at once.

But piece by piece.

And I had no idea how to stop it.

Part 3: When the Unseen Becomes Unbearable

There wasn't a single breaking point.

No explosion. No firefight. No sudden loss that rewrote my life in one shattering second.

What happened to me happened quietly.

It didn't look like trauma. It looked like detachment.

I can't tell you the exact moment I stopped feeling. I only remember realizing, one day, that I hadn't felt anything in a while.

We were on a convoy outside the wire...routine patrol, nothing major. The sun was brutal that morning, baking the air before 8 a.m. I had that familiar layer of sweat already glued beneath my vest. The kind you learn to ignore.

There was a moment when we rolled past a group of children standing barefoot on the edge of the road. One of them smiled at us...maybe ten years old, hand raised like he'd seen Americans wave in movies.

He didn't ask for candy. Didn't beg. Just smiled.

And I didn't wave back.

Not because I was afraid.

Because I didn't care.

That scared me.

I didn't even register it until hours later, after we returned to base. I was sitting on the edge of my bed, peeling off my boots, when the image of his face came back...sunlight bouncing off his face, dust clinging to his eyelashes.

And I realized: *I used to care.*

I used to see children and think of my own.

Now I saw a security risk. A silhouette. A data point.

Something had shifted.

Not snapped.

Eroded.

It wasn't just that moment. It was the accumulation of hundreds like it. The ones you don't think about because you're too tired, too focused, too trained to keep moving.

But the damage adds up.

It shows up in the quiet.

One evening, I was cleaning out my med bag. Restocking supplies, checking my "bleed packs", re-folding wraps that had unraveled during a bumpy ride. Another guy walked by...young, sharp, still carrying some sense of humor. He saw my bag, nodded, and said, "Man, I don't know how you do it. I'd lose it if I had to touch half the crap you've touched."

I just shrugged.

Didn't even look up.

He paused. "You okay, Doc?"

I wanted to say yes.

But what came out was, "Just another day."

He didn't press.

He just nodded and kept walking.

I sat there alone for a few more minutes. Nitrile gloves in one hand, trauma shears in the other. And for some reason, I felt sick.

Not from what I'd seen.

From what I *hadn't* seen.

From the slow loss of empathy. From the way I'd stopped reacting to things that used to move me. From the fact that I couldn't remember the last time I prayed for a patient.

Not because I was angry at God.

Because I was empty.

There's a kind of spiritual starvation that doesn't feel like hunger. It feels like silence.

And I was starving.

I remember trying to explain it to Cathy in a letter I never sent.

I wrote:

"I don't know how to reconcile "here" with "home", Where is God in what I see everyday?… less of me is coming back each day. Like I'm trading little pieces of myself for the ability to keep going. And I don't know what happens when the pieces run out."

I tore the letter up the next morning. She didn't need that. What could she do with it? I was already causing her enough heartache as it is.

But I kept feeling it.

In my body. In my prayers...when I could still form them. In the hollow space where compassion used to live.

You don't always realize what broke until years later...when your kid's watching fireworks and you forget how to breathe with each boom. When someone slams a cabinet and you flinch like the ceiling might cave in. When your wife touches your shoulder in the kitchen and you have to fight the instinct to recoil.

But even then...back there in the desert, in the silence, in the numbness...I knew something had changed.

I wasn't me anymore.

I just didn't know what I was.

Part 4: Grace Didn't Fix It. But It Didn't Leave

There's a common misunderstanding about grace...especially for people raised in faith.

We're taught that grace *fixes* things. That…if we're faithful enough, grace will intervene. It will rescue, repair, return us to something better.

But grace doesn't always work like that.

Sometimes grace doesn't show up with answers.

It just doesn't leave.

There was a night when the FOB was dark for some reason. I don't remember why, maybe a generator issue. But there was a moment between helicopters coming in or out when it was quiet. The silence felt unnatural...almost hostile. I was sitting outside the aid station, staring at nothing, letting the darkness press against my thoughts.

And then someone started to laugh.

Not the forced kind of laugh that soldiers use to keep from crying. A real one. It came from the firepit where we hang out...two guys trading stories about their first cars, I think. Something about how one of them totaled a Chevy Cavalier trying to impress a girl in high school.

They were laughing so hard one of them blew protein shake out his nose.

I didn't join in. But I smiled.

That was the first time I'd smiled in a week.

It wasn't profound. It wasn't a breakthrough. But it broke *something*...just a little. Enough to remind me that even in the fog, even in the numbness, I hadn't completely disappeared.

That's what grace does sometimes. It slips in sideways. In moments you almost overlook.

A week later, I was talking to Cathy and she told me that someone, I don't remember who now, asked today if God is keeping you safe. Cathy had told her yes, even when we don't feel it. She said, "I hope he remembers God is with him."

I read that line over and over. I don't know why it hit me like it did. Maybe because it was so honest. Maybe because it reflected a faith I didn't. Or maybe because it reminded me I was still part of something tender. Something that hadn't been taken.

That night I found myself praying.

Not eloquently. Not even audibly.

Just a whisper in my head: *I don't see You here. But I hope You're still here.*

And I think He was.

Not because anything got better.

But because I felt less alone.

Psalm 34:18 floated back into my mind... "*The Lord is near to the brokenhearted and saves those who are crushed in spirit.*"

I wasn't saved from anything dramatic that day. I was just… seen.

And in that moment, grace wasn't a rescue. It was recognition.

It reminded me that even though I had gone silent, God hadn't.

Even though I didn't feel that I could pray anymore, **Romans 8:26** told me He was still listening: "*We do not know how to pray as we ought, but the Spirit Himself intercedes for us…*"

That verse never felt more true.

Some days I didn't even try. Some days I just sat in the MRAP and looked out at the dust and the crumbled walls and the faces of people I'd never understand, and I would think: *Is this it, Lord? Is this where You are?*

I never heard a voice.

But I never fully gave up, either.

And that's the quiet miracle of grace...it doesn't need your strength to hold on.

It holds you when you forget how.

I didn't return from Afghanistan with a neat testimony or a clean arc. I came back thinner in the soul. Less certain. More fractured. But I also came back with this strange, durable truth:

Cathy didn't leave me…and in that I knew that God didn't leave me.

Not in the fog.

Not in the numbness.

Not in the silence.

And neither did grace.

It didn't shout.

It just stayed.

Part 5: Scripture, Stillness, and the Reflection Hook

If trauma announces itself with noise, erosion happens in stillness.

That's what I learned in Afghanistan. That not every wound bleeds. Some just dissolve you slowly until you're left holding the outline of the man you used to be, wondering when the filling leaked out.

But in that slow unraveling, something unexpected happened.

Scripture returned...not as certainty, but as companionship.

I didn't read it every day. Didn't always understand it. But verses would come to mind like echoes. And they didn't speak in instruction. They spoke in solidarity.

Isaiah 43:2 became one of those verses:

"When you pass through the waters, I will be with you;
and through the rivers, they shall not overwhelm you;
when you walk through fire you shall not be burned,
and the flame shall not consume you."

I didn't feel fireproof. I felt scorched. Thinned out. Weak in places that used to be strong. But somehow...somehow...I hadn't been consumed.

Not entirely.

Not permanently.

Something had held me. Or Someone.

Not because I held on to faith with heroic tenacity. God knows that I didn't.

It was because faith...grace...held on to me.

I used to think faith meant knowing. Now I think it means staying.

I used to think grace came wrapped in healing. Now I know it often comes wrapped in *presence*...the kind that sits with you in the tent, rides with you through the patrol, whispers back to your weariness, *I know. I see. I'm not leaving.*

Grace, I discovered, is not always sweet.

Sometimes it's just **there**.

Sometimes it just keeps showing up, even when you're too numb to notice.

Sometimes it's the sound of laughter a tent over.

Sometimes it's a moth circling a dim light.

Sometimes it's a letter from your daughter, reminding you of a name you haven't heard in months...*Daddy*.

Sometimes it's the Scripture you forgot you memorized, floating back into the fog like a rope tied to something real.

And grace doesn't drag you out.

It anchors you *inside* the storm.

I didn't come back from that year unscarred.

But I came back *held*.

Held through the ache, the silence, the gray.

Held by the God who doesn't always explain...but who *always stays.*

That's what grace actually did.

Reflection Hook for the Reader

Sit with this for a moment:

What's a time in your life that didn't break you all at once...but slowly wore you down?

Not the crisis. The grind. The days that felt like they were taking something from you and you couldn't name what.

What "disconnected" parts of your story still feel silent?

The places you stopped feeling. The pages that went blank. The parts of you that left without fanfare.

Can you name any moments where grace might have stayed, even when you couldn't feel it?

A voice. A verse. A note. A breath. A laugh. A God who stayed even when you forgot how to reach for Him.

Write it down.

Or just let it settle in you.

Grace doesn't need you to resolve it.

It just asks you to recognize where it *never left.*

Part 1: First Morning Back

The first morning home should've been beautiful.

Instead, it felt hollow.

I remember waking up in my own bed...a space I had dreamt about through so many nights of dust, adrenaline, and exhaustion...but it didn't feel like mine. It felt like a borrowed life I wasn't sure how to inhabit anymore. I could hear Cathy doing something in another room, the quiet creak of the a cabinet doors as Cathy grabbed something for the kids.

The sounds were familiar. But they didn't comfort me.

They *startled* me.

Every small noise registered like a potential threat. I was hyperaware but detached...wired for survival in a place built for peace.

When I walked into the kitchen, she smiled.

It was soft. Warm. Honest.

And I didn't know how to return it.

The light coming through the window hit the tile floor just right. I remember noticing how clean everything looked. Too clean. Like a set. Like something from a memory that didn't quite fit anymore.

The kids were there too. Still waking up. Still innocent.

And I was watching all of it like a ghost.

I went through the somewhat like the proverbial zombie until I found it time eat dinner that evening. I sat at the table, and Cathy placed a plate in front of me. But I couldn't eat. Not because I wasn't hungry. Because I didn't know what this act meant anymore.

I thought coming home would fix something.

I thought stepping into this house would be like exhaling after a long breath held in war.

But I didn't feel peace.

I felt… gone.

Like I'd survived something, but left parts of me behind. Like the man who walked into this kitchen was wearing my clothes, drinking my coffee, nodding at his children...but wasn't *me.*

Cathy looked at me across the table. "It's good to have you home," she said.

And I nodded.

Because that's what I was supposed to do.

But inside?

I wasn't home.

Not really.

Not yet.

I looked around and realized something brutal and beautiful at the same time:

The world had kept turning without me.

The kids had grown. Their voices had changed. Cathy's eyes held things I hadn't seen before...strength, yes, but also weariness. A kind of endurance I hadn't asked her to carry, but she had anyway.

They had adapted.

And I… hadn't.

I was still playing catch-up with a life that hadn't paused for me.

And that was the real disorientation.

Not the loudness of war.

The *quiet* of home. This is when I learned what was meant by the expression "The silence was deafening."

There were no helicopters here.

No mortars.

No gunfire.

No late-night adrenaline.

Just a kitchen.

A wife.

And a silence louder than anything I'd faced overseas.

Part 2: The Soundtrack of Disconnection

There's no warning label for what coming home sounds like.

You expect quiet. Rest. Familiarity.

But instead, everything is *off.*

Too loud. Too soft. Too close. Too far.

Fireworks on the Fourth of July should've been a celebration.

Instead, they made my heart sprint like I was back on the FOB during a mortar attack.

The boom of color in the sky wasn't beautiful...it was hostile. My brain knew it was safe. My body didn't get the memo. I clenched the arms of the patio chair until my knuckles went white. Cathy reached out to touch my arm, but even her fingers startled me.

And then there were the moments that *should* have moved me...but didn't.

Like when my son fell and scraped his knee.

I walked over. Picked him up. Dusted him off. Said all the right things.

But inside, I felt… nothing.

I wanted to feel compassion. Alarm. Something.

Instead, there was a blank wall behind my ribs.

I wasn't worried.

I was *absent.*

That scared me more than the fireworks.

Because numbness isn't neutral. It's terrifying.

It tells you something vital is offline, but you don't know how to restart it.

The soundtrack of my days at home was a strange mix...quiet noises that triggered me, and loud emotions I couldn't access.

I'd walk into a grocery store and have to leave because of the crowd. Too many people. Too much noise. I'd fixate on exits, on possible threats, on anyone wearing a hood or standing still too long. I wasn't in Afghanistan anymore, but part of me still lived like I was.

And then there were the nights.

Cathy would lie beside me, her breathing slow, the bedroom dark.

But I couldn't sleep.

And worse...I wanted to reach for her…but didn't know how.

She was glad I was home.

But I wasn't home.

Not really.

Not the way she needed me to be.

Not the way I had promised in the letters and the phone calls and the wishful thinking.

Sometimes I caught her looking at me across the living room with this softness that made me ache...and flinch. Because she was trying. She was still choosing me.

And I didn't know *who* she was choosing anymore.

I didn't know *why* she was choosing me.

I couldn't remember how to let her in.

One afternoon, our oldest climbed into my lap with a book. A familiar story. One I used to read before bedtime with different voices and silly faces.

He handed it to me with that kind of sacred trust only kids can give.

And I froze.

My hands were heavy. My eyes couldn't focus. My mouth felt disconnected from my mind.

I couldn't remember how to be *that* dad.

I opened the book, read a few lines. He waited for the voices. The laughter.

But I just read it straight.

No joy. No warmth.

Just words.

After a minute, he climbed down and wandered off.

He didn't cry.

But something in me did.

Because he wasn't pulling away.

I was.

The house was safe.

The family was loving.

But I was a man who had come home and couldn't figure out how to *re-enter* the life waiting for him.

And the worst part?

No one could hear the dissonance but me.

On the outside, it looked like reunion.

On the inside, it sounded like static.

Part 3: What I Didn't Know I'd Lost

No one tells you what you'll lose when you come home.

Everyone talks about the obvious things...sleep, temper, nerves.

But there's another kind of loss that's harder to name.

You lose *access* to yourself.

You come back with a chest ribbons and a head full of fog, and you sit across from people who love you...and realize that as much as you love them, you've forgotten how to show them.

You've forgotten how to *be known.*

That was the part I wasn't prepared for.

The loneliness wasn't just about them not understanding me.

It was about me not recognizing *myself.*

I'd sit across from Cathy and feel like I was watching our marriage from behind a sheet of glass. I could see her face. Hear her voice. But I couldn't *feel* anything the way I used to. I didn't know how to engage. How to soften. How to stay present without drifting into some inner hallway where the lights flickered and the doors stayed locked.

There were nights she'd ask, "What are you thinking?"

And I'd stare at her.

Not because I didn't want to answer.

But because I didn't *know.*

What do you say when your inner life is all static?

When your memories are jumbled and your emotions are sealed off like a room you closed for the winter and forgot how to warm again?

What do you say when the people around you are ready to love you...and you can't hold it?

I tried to explain a few times.

But the words sounded wrong. Incomplete.

And honestly, even if I could have found the words, part of me was afraid to describe the numbness. Afraid that naming it would make it permanent. Or worse...make them look at me differently.

So I stopped talking.

Started performing.

I did dishes. I took the kids to school. I showed up.

But the man showing up wasn't whole.

He was stitched together just enough to pass.

Just enough to function.

And beneath that surface lived the quiet shame I didn't know what to do with:

"What kind of father doesn't feel joy reading to his kids?"

"What kind of husband doesn't know how to reach for his wife after months apart?"

"What kind of man survives war, only to come home and disappear?"

I wasn't broken like a bone.

I was broken like a compass.

Spinning. Searching.

And when the needle doesn't point anywhere, it's hard to follow anything...including grace.

I started to wonder if I'd lost something essential.

Not my faith exactly. I never doubted God's existence or love for us.

But my *capacity* to feel faith. To rest in it. To trust it.

I had gone through hell and lived.

But what came home wasn't the same man who left.

And no one told me how long it would take to find him again.

Or if I even could.

Part 4: Grace in the Gaps

The hardest part of being home wasn't the fitful sleep, the anxiety, or even the guilt of not being *here.*

It was the *in-between.*

The gaps between moments when I remembered how things used to feel and the reality of how far I still was from feeling them again.

It wasn't really pain.

It was distance.

Like I was in the same room with my family, but behind a glass wall they couldn't see.

They reached for me.

I reached back...mechanically, hesitantly.

And still, grace came.

Not loudly.

Not as some thunderous spiritual awakening.

But in moments so quiet, I almost missed them.

Like the night Cathy sat next to me on the couch. We weren't talking. The TV was on, something forgettable. I was slumped, half-there, still in my own static.

She didn't say anything profound.

She just took my hand.

And left it there.

No squeezing. No asking. No fixing.

Just *being*.

I didn't know how to respond. I didn't even know how to fully feel it. But I knew what it meant.

She wasn't trying to pull me back.

She was telling me she hadn't left.

That's grace.

Another day, my oldest toddled into the room with a plastic figure of some sort and said, "This one is you." He didn't mean anything deep by it. Just a three-year-old assigning identities.

But he handed it to me like it *meant* something.

Like I still had a place.

Like I still belonged.

I remember standing at Mass a few weeks after I came home. I wasn't singing. I wasn't praying. I was just… standing. Watching people close their eyes, lift their hands, whisper their words.

And feeling like I didn't know the language anymore.

Then came the Gospel reading.

"…But while he was still a long way off, his father saw him and was filled with compassion…"
(Luke 15:20)

I had heard that verse a hundred times.

But that day, it didn't sound like a story.

It sounded like a *hope.*

Because I was still a long way off.

From myself. From peace. From joy.

But maybe...just maybe...God had seen me anyway.

And maybe He wasn't waiting at the finish line.

Maybe He was already on the road.

Walking toward me.

Not rushing me.

Not demanding I pull it all together.

Just walking.

Just meeting me in the middle.

That's what grace did in those days.

It didn't erase the numbness.

It *entered* it.

It sat at my breakfast table when I enjoy the meal.

It lay in the bed beside me when I couldn't fall asleep.

It whispered through the pages of a children's book I couldn't read with joy yet.

It wasn't fixing me.

It was *holding* me.

Until I was ready to hold anything again.

Part 5: Reflection and Scripture Integration

For a long time, I thought healing would feel like going back.

Back to who I was. Back to what I remembered. Back to the version of myself who laughed freely, prayed easily, connected without effort.

But healing isn't a return.

It's a reunion...with *God*, with others, and eventually, with the parts of yourself you thought had gone missing for good.

And the thing about reunions?

They rarely happen all at once.

Sometimes, they come in fragments.

In Cathy's hand on mine when I couldn't speak.

In a child's toy dinosaur offered like a peace treaty.

In the moment at Mass when a sentence in Scripture broke through the static.

Grace never demanded I perform for it.

It waited.

Not passively. Not distantly.

But faithfully.

In Psalm 88, the writer confesses:

"You have taken from me friend and neighbor...darkness is my closest friend."

That's where I was, some mornings. Some weeks.

Darkness wasn't just outside me. It was *familiar.*

But grace wasn't scared of that.

It didn't flinch.

Because grace isn't just for the healed.

It's for the ones who aren't sure who they are anymore.

It's for the ones who return home and feel like strangers in their own skin.

It's for the man sitting at his own kitchen table wondering why coffee tastes wrong and why the silence feels louder than any explosion.

That's who God walks toward.

That's who God embraces.

In Isaiah 61, we're told the Spirit of the Lord comes...

"to bind up the brokenhearted... to comfort all who mourn... to bestow on them a crown of beauty instead of ashes..."

He doesn't ask the brokenhearted to clean up first.

He just *binds them.*

Wraps His presence around the jagged edges until something softens.

Until they know: they aren't alone in the ache.

Reflection Hook for the Reader

Maybe you've never been to war. I pray that no one ever does again.

But maybe you know what it's like to come home and not recognize yourself.

Maybe you know the sound of disconnection...the tension between being surrounded by people and still feeling profoundly alone.

If so, take a moment. Ask yourself gently:

What part of you still feels like a stranger to the people who love you?

What do you expect yourself to "be over" by now...but still aren't?

And where might grace be waiting for you?

Not with a lecture. Not with a timeline.

Just with a chair across from yours, a quiet hand on your shoulder, and the soft, steady reminder:

"Even if you don't feel like you anymore...I still see you. I'm still here."

Part 1: The Day It Happened

The call came in like they always do...crackling, clipped, chaotic.

IED.

Multiple casualties. Two critically wounded.

The kind of report you train for and pray you'll never answer.

We were already moving before the last word finished.

Boots on gravel. Gear slung. Voices sharp, restrained. Everyone knew the drill, but there was no autopilot for this. Every movement was precise, every heartbeat a little louder.

The sun was high, but everything felt shadowed.

Dust swirled in the air before we even saw the helicopter.

Two soldiers were pulled from the helo, limp, unconscious. Another medic was already performing CPR on one of them.

Mike Metcalf.

Jonathan Walsh.

I'll never forget how small they looked on those litters.

Walsh had already been called as gone. Mike was on the table.

Shirt cut open. IVs started. Breathing tube inserted.

I didn't have time to think.

My hands moved the way they always had...assist, provide what the surgeon needs. The OR was a storm of voices and instruments and blood. And in the middle of it, one man whose life was slipping away like water through our fingers.

We were already beginning a full thoracotomy on Mike. I don't remember who said it first...one of the surgeons, maybe the anesthetist after a shock from the defibrillator.

"We got a response."

We worked harder. Find the issue, stitch it, seal it or otherwise, another unit of blood. Defib pads. Barked orders that almost didn't sound like English anymore. As if volume could bend death backward.

I remember checking for a pulse.

Nothing.

That silence that isn't silence at all...it's finality.

And then came the stillness.

Everyone just… stopped.

There's a kind of holy hush in the OR when the fight ends and death wins.

You don't cry. You don't scream.

You just feel everything inside you go still.

I stood there, blood on my gloves, sweat soaking through my uniform, and stared at the body that had been alive thirty minutes ago. Two men who had laughed that morning. Maybe thought about lunch. Maybe prayed. Maybe didn't.

Now they were gone.

And nothing in me could make sense of it.

This wasn't cinematic.

It wasn't noble or tragic or dramatic.

It was brutal.

Real.

And it wouldn't let go.

Their names didn't fade like some casualty report.

They *stuck*.

Mike Metcalf.

Jonathan Walsh.

I carried their blood under my fingernails for days.

I carry their names on my soul to this day.

And even now, every time I hear the word "freedom," I remember the sounds in the operating room. The smell of antiseptic, blood, sweat and loss. The suddenness with which life can be taken.

And how sacred the remembering is.

Part 2: In the OR – Where Bodies and Souls Pass Through

They don't tell you, in training, how much of the job is holding space for death.

You learn the procedures. The tourniquets. The triage protocols. How to move fast, how to move clean. You practice bleeding simulations, chest tubes, mass casualties. You know what to do when a body's failing.

But nothing prepares you for when a soul is leaving.

The Field Surgical Hospital wasn't a place for poetry. It was fluorescent lights, plywood walls, stainless steel, and constant motion. But on the days someone died, it felt like a chapel. A brutal, blood-soaked, holy chapel.

When Mike and Jonathan were brought in, everything in the room snapped tight.

The surgeons barked.

The nurses flew into motion.

Everyone had a role. No space for hesitation.

But even with adrenaline pumping, my heart slowed.

There was this split-second, right before my gloved hands touched Mike's chest, where time dilated.

I looked at his face.

He wasn't completely gone yet.

But he wasn't there, either.

His eyes were open, unfocused. Like they were trying to find something. Or someone.

There's a kind of panic that happens inside you when you realize you're standing between a man and the end of his story...and you're not enough to stop it.

My hands worked, but my chest was caving in.

I could hear the suction. The beeping. Someone cursing under their breath. The clatter of instruments being passed and dropped and wiped clean again. And beneath it all, this awful knowing:

We were going to lose him.

The room was packed, but I felt alone. Like I was standing in a doorway no one wanted to acknowledge...a place where flesh fails and something eternal happens, whether we're ready or not.

What does it mean to be there when someone dies?

To be the last set of hands that touched them?

To be the witness, the vessel, the one who keeps breathing?

I don't remember crying.

Not then.

You can't.

You compartmentalize. You shove it down. You move to the next patient. You start to clean the OR, readying it for the next casualt and your thoughts.

But later...later it all echoes back.

The antiseptic smell mixed with blood. The faint chemical smell of explosives or diesel fuel.

The pressure of your palms on a man's chest who will never see his daughter again.

The way no one says it out loud, but everyone knows:

We lost two brothers today.

And there is no comfort big enough to answer that.

But there is something else.

Something quieter.

Something I've only come to call grace.

It wasn't peace. Not yet.

It was presence.

It was Cathy's voice on a call that night, when I didn't have words, and she didn't ask for any.

It was the fact that even in death, those men weren't treated like bodies.

They were *honored.*

Their names were spoken.

Their faces remembered.

Their blood not sanitized away as data or consequence, but *witnessed.*

That, I've learned, is holy.

To be the one who watches.

To be the one who *won't forget.*

To be the one who says: "I was there. And they mattered."

Part 3: The Question That Won't Let Go – "Why Them?"

I didn't ask it out loud at first.

But it lived in me.

Why them?

Why not me?

I was still here.

Still walking.

Still waking up.

Still trying to make peace with breath.

I've heard people call that *survivor's guilt.*

But guilt is too clinical a word for what it feels like in your chest. I wasn't in the vehicle when it was hit. I wasn't even in these men's unit.

It's not just a sadness.

It's a *disorientation*...like you got the math wrong and can't show your work.

There were others, too. Scott Pace. Matthew Fazzari who's helicopter had been shot down but came into the FST barely alive…names I heard over the radio or saw on casualty lists. Some I knew. Some I didn't.

Some were in the wrong place at the wrong time.

Some did everything right...and died anyway.

Others made mistakes and somehow survived.

That's the part that haunts you.

It's not just that they're gone.

It's that their deaths *don't make sense.*

I've seen men walk away from blasts that should've killed them.

And I've seen men die of wounds or accidents that they shouldn't have.

Why do children suffer and die for the actions and war of adults.

Why did we regular see children coughing up blood, dying of tuberculosis…an illness not even seen at home?

You can't theologize that.

You can't reason your way through it with platitudes or logic or systems of fairness.

There is no chart.

There is no formula.

There is only the question that sits in the pit of your soul:

"Why me, Lord?"

Kris Kristofferson put it bluntly.

And I've whispered it more than once.

Not just in grief...but in disbelief.

What is the rationale for living and dying?

Am I living on borrowed time?

If so, what am I supposed to do with this borrowed time?

And what if I waste it?

That's the part no one tells you about.

My inability to reconcile all of this didn't just ache...it *accused.*

It said, "You owe them something."

But what?

A perfect life?

A flawless recovery?

A testimony worth their absence?

I've tried.

I've spoken their names.

I've told their stories.

I've written and prayed and worked and served.

But still...some nights...the question sits with me.

Unanswered. Unresolved.

Why them?

And the truth?

Grace hasn't answered it.

But it hasn't *left me* alone with it, either.

Part 4: When Grace Meant Staying Human

There's a temptation, after too many losses, to go cold.

You don't plan it. It just happens.

You get good at the movements...treat the injury, wash the blood, mark the chart. You say the names with flat affect. You nod at memorials but stop making eye contact. You don't cry, because you're not sure when you'd stop if you started.

That's the drift: from human to function.

From brother to body.

From witness to technician.

I came close to that edge more than once.

I could feel it...this slow hardening, this emotional frost climbing up my ribs. I knew that if I crossed into numbness, I might never come back.

And that's when grace showed up...not to comfort me, but to *keep me human.*

Grace didn't rescue me from the grief.

It *tethered* me to it.

It reminded me that grief isn't weakness.

It's proof I still felt.

Still loved.

Still remembered.

One night, weeks after I returned, I was sitting in the dark, just... holding it all. The faces. The guilt. The noise. The silence.

Cathy walked into the room, saw me hunched forward, and didn't say a word.

She just sat down next to me.

Not to fix.

Not to question.

Just to be there.

That was grace.

Not through words.

Through presence.

Later, I would talk to the VA shrink. I didn't go to him for answers...I didn't believe in them anymore. I went because I didn't want to be alone with the ache.

I told him about Mike's eyes. The way they stared but didn't see. The way I keep seeing them, over and over, when I close mine.

He didn't try to explain it away.

He just said, "Maybe the reason you remember is because it matters that *someone does.*"

That landed in a place I didn't know was open.

It matters that I still say their names.

It matters that I remember the heroic efforts of the surgical team and my fellow medics.

It matters that I still flinch at fireworks and pause when I hear a name I haven't heard in years.

Because that's grace too...not forgetting.

Not allowing death to turn real people into memory foam silhouettes.

Not turning sacred lives into statistics.

Grace says: *you're still allowed to feel this.*

You're allowed to mourn *again*, even if everyone else has moved on.

You're allowed to carry their names like an ache in your soul...not as a wound, but as a *witness.*

Because if we lose our capacity to feel, we lose our capacity to love.

And if we lose that, what exactly are we surviving for?

Grace didn't give me peace about their deaths…I still struggle with reconciling the seemingly randomness of it.

But it kept me from going silent.

It taught me that maybe, staying human was the greatest way I could honor them.

Not because I'm strong.

But because I'm still *soft* in the places that matter.

Part 5: Reflection and Scripture Integration

Some days, it still feels unreal.

That I was there. That they're not.

That I came home to birthdays and backyard cookouts while their families sat at folded tables under a funeral tent.

I used to think faith meant having answers for that.

Now I know faith is what keeps you *present* when there aren't any.

The more I've sat with the ache and confusion of reconciling it all, the more I've come to believe that grace doesn't compete with grief. It doesn't ask you to get over it. It doesn't say, *"Be grateful...it could have been worse."*

Grace *names* the fallen.

Grace holds their stories.

Grace lets you keep their laughter close without needing to justify why it still breaks your heart.

Jesus once said:

"Greater love has no one than this: to lay down one's life for one's friends."
...John 15:13

And that's what they did.

Mike. Scott. Jonathan. Matthew. So many others.

They laid down their lives in a place where most people wouldn't even choose to visit.

And I get to *live.*

Not as a repayment.

But as a response.

Their names echo in everything I do now.

Not out of guilt.

Out of *gratitude*...the kind that bleeds.

There's a verse in Revelation, spoken like a whisper over the future:

"He will wipe away every tear from their eyes. There will be no more death or mourning or crying or pain…"
...Revelation 21:4

I believe that.

Not because I always feel it.

But because some days, it's the only promise that keeps me soft enough to remember.

And that remembering...it's holy.

"There is a time to weep, and a time to laugh. A time to mourn, and a time to dance…"
...Ecclesiastes 3:1–4

I used to think those were different seasons.

Now I know they overlap.

You can laugh while you mourn.

You can hold joy and sorrow in the same breath.

You can stand in church on a Sunday morning and still feel a tremor of loss when a flag waves during the song.

That doesn't mean you're broken.

It means you're *human.*

And grace...real grace...lets you stay that way.

Reflection Hook for the Reader

Pause with me here.

Not to move past the grief...but to make space for it.

Who are the people in your life you've lost...but haven't forgotten?

What names still echo in your soul, even when the world has gone quiet about them?

Where have you been carrying sorrow in silence, believing no one could understand?

Let this be your reminder:

You don't have to let go to move forward.

You don't have to explain your grief to justify its weight.

And you don't have to silence your sorrow to honor your faith.

Grace doesn't remove the ache.

It gives it *dignity.*

So speak their names.

Remember the moments.

And trust that God has never forgotten them either.

Part 1: Fireworks and Flashbacks

It was the Fourth of July.

The sky was clear. The grill was hot. The kids had face paint and sparklers and a kind of joy that only exists when you're too young to understand what explosives can mean to someone who's seen the real thing.

I should have been laughing.

Instead, I was scanning for exits.

One pop, that's all it took.

Just one.

The kind of firework that sounds more like a concussion than a celebration. Deep, low, guttural. It echoed off the trees in the backyard and punched something loose in my chest.

My whole body froze.

Sweat beaded on my neck, but I wasn't moving.

Just staring at the sky like it had betrayed me.

My eyes darted...where's the source? Is it incoming? Where's the nearest cover? Where are the kids?

I crouched without thinking.

Instinct, not logic.

I heard a voice call my name...Cathy's, I think...but it was muffled, far away. Like I was underwater. Like I had slipped into another timeline and couldn't find the exit ramp back.

And then, I heard a baby cry. My daughter.

That pulled me back like a hook in the ribs.

I took her from my wife's arms and muttered something about taking her to the car to get out of the noise…that I didn't mind missing the show.

Shut the car door.

Stared at myself in the windshield.

Hands shaking.

Not from fear.

From *fury*.

"What the hell is wrong with me?"

That was the only sentence in my head.

I was a trained combat medic. I'd seen real explosions. Real bodies. Real death.

And here I was, hiding from fireworks in the middle of Dallas, Texas.

This wasn't the man I had promised Cathy would come back.

This wasn't the dad my kids deserved.

But it was the truth.

I hadn't brought the war home in my duffel bag.

It had come home in *me*.

It lived in the corners of my mind I couldn't sweep clean.

It flared up in grocery stores, when someone dropped something behind me.

It whispered at night, keeping my chest tight and my eyes open long after everyone else was asleep.

PTSD wasn't a label I wanted.

It sounded like a diagnosis for someone else.

Someone weak. Someone unstable.

But that day sitting in the car, hiding from a fireworks show, I couldn't lie anymore.

I had survived Afghanistan.

But I was still fighting a war no one could see.

Part 2: The Wreckage You Didn't Expect

I came home with all my limbs intact.

But something inside me had splintered.

And not in one, dramatic break.

More like cracks that spread slowly across the glass of my life...barely visible at first, until everything began to feel fragile.

Sleep was the first thing to go.

When it did come, it wasn't restful. It was fractured, haunted, interrupted by the smallest sounds...a creak in the floor, a gust of wind, Cathy turning over in bed. I'd jolt awake, heart racing, drenched in sweat, unsure of what year it was.

Other nights, I couldn't fall asleep at all.

I'd sit in the living room, the TV on, staring at the soft flicker of late-night commercials like they were some kind of static lullaby. Anything to distract me from the reel playing behind my eyes.

Crowds became unbearable. Grocery stores. Churches. Any big event.

I'd walk into a room and start scanning.

Exits. Blind spots. Backpacks left unattended.

My mind rewrote every environment into a threat map.

I couldn't shut it off.

Even in the safest places, my body didn't believe I was safe.

Cathy noticed, of course.

She'd reach for my hand during Mass, and I'd flinch.

Not because I didn't love her.

Because I couldn't *feel* love in those moments.

It was like the wiring in me had changed. Emotions came in jumbled...too fast, too flat, too much, or not at all.

She tried to understand.

She really did.

But nothing about PTSD is linear. One day I was fine, taking the kids to school and making dinner. The next, I was leaving the grocery store early, leaving Cathy to finish on her own.

The worst part wasn't the panic.

It was the helplessness.

Watching Cathy carry the weight of my silence, my mood swings, my cold detachment...and not being able to stop it.

I saw her face when I told the kids we couldn't go to a concert in the park.

I saw her shrink a little, saw the frown of disappointment.

I wasn't the only one in pain.

But I was the one creating it.

And that truth dug deep.

I was supposed to be the protector. The stable one. The guy who made things better, not heavier.

Instead, I was a walking minefield.

And my family kept stepping on the triggers I didn't even know were there.

Cathy never accused me. Never yelled.

But her eyes asked questions I couldn't answer.

"Are you still in there?"

"Will I ever get my husband back?"

I didn't know.

All I knew was that I couldn't fake normal anymore.

Not in this house.

Not with these kids.

Not with the woman who had stayed when she could have walked.

I came home hoping everything would be okay.

But I hadn't expected this kind of wreckage.

The kind that leaves no debris on the floor.

Only distance.

Only silence.

Only the constant, crushing realization that surviving isn't the same as healing.

And maybe, just maybe, it was time to admit I needed something more than grit to keep going.

Part 3: The Moment You Knew You Needed Help

There wasn't a single moment that broke me.

It was more like the floor giving out in stages.

But there *was* a moment when I finally stopped pretending.

It was a Saturday.

The kids had been fighting over something...some loud, ordinary squabble about who got the last pancake. Nothing out of the norm. But my nerves were already frayed. I hadn't slept. I'd had that dream again, the one with the girl that lost her legs.

And then the plate dropped.

Just a regular plate, slipping off the counter and shattering on the kitchen floor.

I lost it.

I didn't hit anyone. I didn't throw anything.

I just walked out of the house and stayed there for a while, heart racing.

I didn't know if anyone noticed. It wouldn't have mattered regardless.

Cathy didn't follow. I now know she instead had to make excuses to the kids on where I went.

I stood there, chest heaving, ashamed to breathe.

Later that night, I sat alone on the back porch.

The cicadas were loud. The stars were bright. And I felt like I was a thousand miles away from all of it.

That's when Cathy came out.

She sat down next to me, hands folded, quiet.

Then, with a voice so soft it almost didn't reach me, she asked:

"How are you going to live that way?"

I didn't answer.

Because I knew.

I had known for months.

But this time, I couldn't dodge the question.

I couldn't shift the blame or make excuses or act like everything was manageable.

I wasn't managing.

I was imploding in slow motion.

And the people I loved most were standing too close.

I nodded.

That was the moment grace got in.

Not through healing.

Through *surrender.*

I still thought admitting I was broken made me weak.

But the truth?

That's where healing starts.

When you stop pretending you're fine and say the words that scare you most:

"I can't do this alone."

And you don't have to.

Part 4: Healing Didn't Come Quickly...but Grace Came Quietly

I went to the VA and was sent to a discussion group. But I couldn't relate to the guys there. They were suffering worse that I was, unable to function in daily life. This made me feel worse, not better.

So I went to another, private shrink for an initial visit.

I sat across from a woman who looked too kind to understand what I had seen. But then she asked, "When do you feel like you stopped feeling?" and something in my throat tightened.

I didn't answer right away.

But I didn't leave, either.

That was a beginning.

We didn't dive into trauma on the first day. Or the fifth. Or even the tenth. She taught me to name what I was experiencing...I wasn't the stereotype (no hypervigilance, no moral injury). Mine wasn't a single event but the accumulation of those we helped and lost. She gave language to what had, until then, only been reactions. She didn't rush me toward healing. She made space for the wound to breathe.

Healing was uneven.

Some mornings I felt like progress.

Others, I didn't.

But grace didn't measure my worth in consistency.

It met me in *presence.*

In the laugh of one of my kids when I least expected it...sharp and wild and so normal that it brought tears to my eyes.

In the Eucharist, even when I felt numb...standing there with nothing to offer, and still being fed.

In Cathy's patience, which didn't come with ultimatums. She didn't expect me to "get better." She just wanted me to be *honest.* And she kept showing up, even when I had nothing to give back.

One night, I couldn't sleep again. The anxiety was back...tight chest, restless legs. I walked into the living room and just stood there, staring at the wall.

No prayers came. No words.

Just this sense that *I'm still here.*

That was grace too.

It didn't shout.

It didn't cure.

It just sat with me in the dark.

The verse I had avoided for years started circling back:

"My grace is sufficient for you, for My power is made perfect in weakness."
...2 Corinthians 12:9

I didn't want to need grace in my weakness.

I wanted to be strong again.

But maybe that was never the goal.

Maybe grace wasn't waiting for the old me to return.

Maybe grace had stayed *with* me in the wreckage...and was willing to walk at the speed I could handle.

Some days, healing looked like praying again.

Other days, it looked like *not* isolating.

Some days, it was showing up to Mass.

Other days, it was just not yelling.

It wasn't linear. It wasn't fast.

But it was *real.*

And it reminded me...slowly, painfully...that healing doesn't come when you *feel* strong.

It begins the moment you *tell the truth.*

Part 5: Reflection and Scripture Integration

I used to think grace was for the moment you got it together.

Now I know grace is for the moment you fall apart.

Not dramatic collapse...just the daily unraveling of a soul trying to stay upright through triggers, memories, tension, and noise no one else can hear.

PTSD didn't just live in my mind.

It lived in my marriage. In my children's eyes. In the way I stood near doorways and hated crowded restaurants. In how I apologized for the same thing over and over: not being fully there.

But grace kept showing up.

Not with fixes.

With *faithfulness.*

In *Psalm 147:3*, it says:

"He heals the brokenhearted and binds up their wounds."

That verse used to sound gentle.

Now it sounds *messy.*

Because healing a heart isn't like stitching a cut. It's long. It's complicated. It reopens. It resists.

But the binding...it keeps happening.

God doesn't ask me to be whole before He loves me.

He *binds* what's broken. Even when it's breaking again.

And in *Romans 8:26*, Paul writes:

"The Spirit helps us in our weakness. For we do not know what to pray for as we ought…"

That was me, night after night.

I didn't know how to pray.

So grace prayed in the silence.

In the exhausted breath.

Grace lets me love my family, not perfectly, but honestly.

Grace reminds me I'm not failing them...I'm just fighting a war they can't see.

But I'm not fighting it alone anymore.

Reflection Hook for the Reader

You may not have worn a uniform.

But maybe you've come home from something that changed you.

And maybe you're still fighting something nobody else sees.

So pause with this:

What are the silent battles you fight that no one else sees?

Where have you resisted help...even when grace was trying to reach you?

What would it cost you to be honest...for the first time in a long time?

This isn't about shame.

It's about truth.

Healing doesn't ask for perfection.

It asks for permission.

Let grace begin there.

Part 1: A Quiet Moment at Home

It was a Tuesday. Or maybe a Thursday. One of those slow, gray mornings where nothing special was on the calendar. The house was still waking up. I was sitting in the corner of the couch in one of my old T-shirts that Cathy hates.

Cathy came in holding a Monster (I'm not a coffee drinker).

She didn't say anything at first...just set the drink down on the table beside me. No ceremony. No speech. She'd brought it, even though I hadn't asked. Even though I'd been grumpy the night before. Even though I'd been quiet that morning.

She just… *brought it.*

Then she went back to the kitchen, humming something under her breath.

And I sat there looking at that cup like it was holy.

Because in that moment, I realized something:

It wasn't a grand gesture. It was grace...in sweatpants.

Nothing about it made headlines. No Instagram quote could capture it.

But it was love.

Still warm.

Still being offered.

Still here.

A few minutes later, one of the kids wandered in...half-asleep, hair sticking up, dragging a blanket behind them like it owed them rent. They didn't say good morning. They just climbed up next to me, curled into my side, and exhaled.

That was it.

That was the whole moment.

But something sacred cracked open in me.

They didn't need a speech.

They didn't need an explanation.

They didn't need me to be impressive or healed or strong.

They just needed *me.*

And somehow...despite everything...I was still here.

That was grace too.

Not the kind that lifts you out of despair.

The kind that quietly *stays* through it.

The kind that shows up on an ordinary Tuesday and brings you coffee before you've earned it.

The kind that curls into your side without needing you to speak.

For years, I had looked for grace in dramatic moments...conversion, rescue, some mountaintop sign that I was okay again.

But it turns out, grace wasn't always dramatic.

Sometimes it just a drink.

Sat beside me.

And *didn't leave.*

That's when I realized: I'd been measuring grace by how much I felt it.

But grace wasn't always a feeling.

Sometimes, grace was just this:

You're still here. And they are too.

Part 2: What Cathy Carried

I didn't know, at the time, how much I was asking of her.

In those months...maybe even years...after I came home, I was functioning just enough to fool everyone else. But not Cathy. She saw it. The stiffness in my hugs. The delayed reactions. The empty eyes when the kids were laughing.

She knew before I did that something was deeply wrong.

And still, she stayed.

Not because she didn't have the right to leave.

But because she had already *decided* to stay.

I wish I could say I made it easy.

But I didn't.

There were nights I came to bed and barely said a word.

Days I drifted through the house like a fog.

Arguments that weren't even arguments...just emotional cold fronts blowing through our living room with no explanation and no apology.

She tried asking me what I needed.

Some days I said "nothing." Most days, I didn't know.

And yet…

She kept going..

She packed the lunches.

She took the kids to church when I couldn't bring myself to go.

She carried the rhythms of our life like they were a sacred vow.

Because to her, they were.

That's what grace looked like.

Not ease.

Not answers.

But endurance.

I remember one day, months into the worst of it, I wanted to leave shopping early due to the crowds.

She just looked at me. Eyes full, but not angry.

And she said, "I know you're trying. But I'm still here."

That sentence broke something in me.

Because she didn't say, *"Figure it out."*

She said, *"I love you."*

She held the line when I had nothing left.

She wasn't waiting for the man she married to come back.

She was loving the man who was standing in front of her...even when he was mostly shadow.

That kind of love?

It's not flashy.

It doesn't get thanked enough.

But it saved something in me I didn't know was still alive.

She didn't rescue me.

She didn't need to.

She just stayed.

And that saved something too.

I once heard someone say that grace doesn't always pull you out of the pit.

Sometimes, it just *climbs in and sits beside you.*

That was Cathy.

Grace, in human form.

Not solving me.

Just refusing to leave me.

Part 3: God Didn't Leave Either

There were long stretches when I didn't pray.

Not really.

I knew the words. I could go through the motions. But the space between me and God felt thick...like shouting into fog. I'd sit at Mass and hear the readings, and part of me would nod, but deeper down, something would whisper, *Where were You?*

I never stopped believing in God.

But I *did* start wondering if He had stopped believing in me.

Not out of anger. Out of absence.

I thought faith meant *feeling* His presence.

But what happens when all you feel is tired?

Numb?

Alone?

I remember one Sunday, sitting in the back row of church. The toddlers were fidgeting, Cathy was wrangling crayons and fruit snacks, and I was barely holding my composure. The priest read the Gospel...*something about the lost sheep, or maybe the prodigal son, I don't know*...but then the line came:

"While he was still a long way off, his father saw him and was filled with compassion."
...Luke 15:20

I didn't cry.

I didn't move.

But something inside me loosened.

Because that was *me.*

A long way off.

Still walking, still unsure if I belonged, if I'd ever be whole again.

But somehow… still *seen.*

I couldn't conjure the feeling of being held by God.

But I was starting to believe I hadn't been *let go.*

Maybe grace wasn't the lightning bolt I kept waiting for.

Maybe it was the quiet breath I took in the morning.

The steady voice of Cathy whispering prayers I'd forgotten how to say.

The toddler grabbing my hand mid-Mass and grinning like everything was okay.

Maybe grace isn't always what pulls you *out* of the pit.

Maybe it's who sits *in* it with you.

In *Psalm 139*, the psalmist asks:

"Where can I go from Your Spirit? Where can I flee from Your presence? If I make my bed in the depths, You are there."

There were nights I had made my bed in those depths.

And still, something held me together.

Not by explaining everything.

But by not leaving.

God didn't shout through the darkness.

He just didn't leave the room.

Part 4: Reflection and Scripture Integration

If I had to name the kind of grace that saved me, I wouldn't point to a miracle.

I'd point to a Tuesday morning.

I'd point to a Monster Energy placed gently on the table without a word.

I'd point to the sound of crayons rolling across a church pew.

To the way a child crawled into my lap and didn't ask for an explanation...just presence.

To Cathy's sigh in the hallway after a long day, not because she had given up, but because she hadn't.

To the way God didn't shout answers from the sky...but somehow stayed in the silence.

That's what *stayed.*

Not certainty. Not clarity. Not always hope.

But love.

The kind that doesn't leave the room when things get hard.

The kind that's described in *Lamentations 3:22–23*:

"The steadfast love of the Lord never ceases; His mercies never come to an end; they are new every morning."

That verse used to feel distant...like something embroidered on a pillow in a house where people don't fall apart.

But now?

Now it sounds like Cathy's footsteps in the kitchen at 6 a.m.

It sounds like the rustle of little feet climbing into my bed before dawn.

It sounds like *presence.*

Like *persistence.*

Like love that doesn't give up when it's tired, or frustrated, or afraid.

1 Corinthians 13:7 says it plainly:

"Love bears all things, believes all things, hopes all things, endures all things."

That's not abstract.

That's a woman who chose to stay.

That's a child who reached without fear.

That's a God who didn't disappear when I stopped praying.

That's grace.

And it *stayed.*

Even when I didn't.

Even when I couldn't.

Even when I wasn't sure I wanted it to.

Grace never walked out.

And now, looking back?

I think that's the only reason I made it home at all.

Reflection Hook for the Reader

So let me ask you:

Who are the people who stayed with you...even when you didn't deserve it?

What quiet graces are present in your life right now that you've been too hurt or too busy to notice?

Can you begin to see the hand of God...not in the miracles you've been waiting for, but in the people who haven't left your side?

This chapter isn't a call to be strong.

It's a reminder that you're not alone.

You never were.

Part 1: A Normal Day That Looked Different

It was nothing special.

I was sitting in traffic, hands on the wheel, some generic country song humming low from the radio...one of the ones that used to roll right off me. The sun was low, hitting the windshield just wrong. My phone buzzed in the passenger seat, ignored. A school bus passed by in the opposite lane.

And then, I saw it.

Not a vision. Not a sign. Just… a couple of kids on the sidewalk.

The older one was crouched down, zipping her sister's coat. The little one laughed and leaned into her sister's neck as the zipper caught her chin.

It was such a simple thing.

So normal.

But for the first time in what felt like forever, I *noticed it.*

Not with analysis. Not with distance.

With a kind of clarity I hadn't felt in years.

And the words that floated through me weren't deep theology or some grand realization.

They were just:

"I see it now."

I don't know when it started.

There wasn't a ceremony. No lightning bolt. Just these quiet, accumulating moments where the world began to take color again.

Where the haze I'd been walking through started to thin. Where beauty, the kind I had stopped looking for, started waving back.

It had been so long since I'd really *seen* anything that wasn't a threat.

For years, my eyes had scanned the world in analysis mode?

But that morning?

Those girls?

That laugh?

It was *grace.*

Not loud. Not heroic.

Just present.

There was a time when I couldn't even notice joy, much less feel it.

But something had shifted.

And I don't mean I was healed.

I wasn't.

I was still jumpy in crowds.

Still bracing at fireworks.

Still carrying the scars of things no one should've had to see.

But this?

This was different.

It wasn't like flipping on a light.

It was more like remembering I had eyes.

The world hadn't changed.

But my *vision* had.

That's what grace had been doing all along...slowly, patiently, invisibly...healing not just what I felt, but how I *saw*.

Not just the battlefield.

But the *beauty*.

Not just the loss.

But what *remained*.

Part 2: Grace Changes Your Vision Before It Changes Your Life

The pain didn't leave.

The images didn't vanish.

The nights didn't always bring rest.

But I started noticing things again...things that had been there the whole time but were invisible to me through the fog of trauma, survival, and self-protection.

Grace didn't start by fixing the story.

It started by *changing how I saw it.*

At first, it felt small...almost inconsequential. Like the way the light came through our kitchen window in the morning and landed on Cathy's face. Or how my youngest, still in pajamas, danced to a cereal jingle like it was Beethoven. Or how my older two kids, once awkward and quiet around me, started dropping one-liners again at the dinner table...testing the waters, trying to pull me into the rhythm of our family like I hadn't missed a beat.

I started seeing them.

Not just observing. *Seeing.*

Before grace touched my eyes, I saw everything through utility and analysis.

What needs to get done?

Where's the threat?

What do I need to manage?

But grace started peeling back the layers of my lens.

And suddenly, I began to notice that pain wasn't just in me.

It was in others.

The tired cashier whose smile didn't reach her eyes.

The coworker who laughed too hard and too fast, trying to hide something.

The guy in the pew in front of me at Mass, who didn't stand for the Gospel reading...and looked like he was holding back tears the entire time.

I didn't look away anymore.

Grace made me *slower to judge*...because I had felt the sting of being misunderstood. It made me *quieter*...not because I didn't have opinions, but because I had learned the weight of silence.

And maybe the biggest shift?

I started to believe that God hadn't wasted my pain.

That the story I was ashamed of… the story I'd tried to push down and edit into something cleaner… might actually matter to someone else.

Maybe I hadn't survived *just* to survive.

Maybe I'd survived to *see differently.*

That verse from *Isaiah 42:16* started coming to mind:

"I will lead the blind by ways they have not known, along unfamiliar paths I will guide them."

I had walked those unfamiliar paths. Blind, most of the way.

But now?

Now I was beginning to believe that blindness wasn't the end.

That grace wasn't just about saving me from disaster.

It was about slowly giving me the ability to notice *what matters most.*

The beauty.

The brokenness.

The invitations.

I wasn't "back to normal." I never would be.

But I had begun to *see* again.

And that changed everything...even before anything around me did.

Part 3: The World Started Looking Like a Mission Field Again

I wasn't looking to start anything.

I wasn't hunting for a cause.

Honestly, I was just trying to keep my days stitched together. Trying not to sink back into the numbness. Trying to hold conversations without drifting. Trying to sleep through the night without the ceiling fan sounding like rotor blades.

But something had shifted.

One afternoon, I was standing at Home Depot...staring at screws I didn't need, and I overheard a guy behind me talking on the phone. He wasn't being loud. But he wasn't hiding his frustration, either.

"...I told her I don't know what else to say. I can't feel anything anymore. I don't even know what I'm doing here."

He hung up and stood there...just frozen.

Not angry. Not even visibly upset.

Just… *lost.*

I didn't know him.

But something in me pulsed.

I knew that tone. That numbness. That slow, quiet collapse under the weight of invisible things.

I didn't do anything grand. I just made eye contact. Nodded. Said something dumb like, "Rough day?"

He looked surprised. Then he nodded back.

We stood there, neither of us saying much. But it was enough.

That's when I realized: **I was starting to see people again.** Not as strangers to ignore. But as mirrors.

And grace didn't let me keep looking away.

Another time, a friend reached out...someone I hadn't talked to in months. Said he was going through a rough stretch and asked if we could get together. I almost said no. The kids had practice. I was tired. I didn't feel wise or ready.

But something inside me whispered, *You've walked where he's standing. Show up.*

So I did.

And we didn't solve anything. But we talked. And when he cried, I didn't flinch.

I just let the moment be heavy.

Because I'd learned how to sit in that weight.

Not as a counselor. Definitely, not as a preacher.

Just as someone who *knows.*

That's what grace had been doing...turning my wounds into a kind of lens. A way to see others not as projects, but as people who, like me, were still carrying something unspoken.

I used to think God used people after they were healed.

Now I think He just uses the ones who *see.*

2 Kings 6:17 tells the story of Elisha's servant panicking over an approaching enemy army, and Elisha prays:

"Open his eyes, Lord, so that he may see."

Not *rescue him.*

Not *give him strength.*

Open his eyes.

That's what happened to me.

The war didn't leave.

The pain didn't vanish.

But the *mission* changed.

It wasn't about saving people.

It was about *noticing them.*

It was about showing up for the people grace pointed out...because grace always sees the hurting.

And now?

So do I.

Part 4: I Don't See Perfectly. But I See…and I try.

There are still days when the fog rolls back in.

Still mornings I sit at the edge of my bed, trying to remember why I'm supposed to get up.

Still nights when my skin flinches at a sudden sound, and my mind launches into defense mode before I even know what's happening.

The scars didn't leave.

They just stopped being the only thing I could see.

Grace didn't erase the damage.

It taught me how to *live with vision in the midst of it.*

There's a difference.

I used to think healing would mean everything went quiet...the triggers, the guilt, the looping memories.

But that silence never came.

What did come, eventually, was something softer. A kind of alertness. A new orientation.

I started waking up...not just in body, but in awareness.

Seeing my wife's face across the kitchen table, not just as the woman who held the house together, but as the one who *stayed* through every cracked version of me.

Seeing my kids...not as extensions of my obligation, but as proof that grace still multiplies through presence.

Even seeing myself...not as a project, not as a failure...but as someone worth *bringing back.*

There's a moment in the Gospel of John, when a man who had been blind from birth is healed by Jesus. The Pharisees swarm him with theological questions, trying to dissect his experience. And all he says is:

"I was blind. And now I see."
...John 9:25

That's how it feels.

I can't explain the timeline.

Can't map the process.

Can't trace it to a single therapy session or Scripture or Sunday.

But somewhere along the way...through tears, through silence, through sifting the ashes of my story...

I realized I was *seeing again.*

Not perfectly.

Not always clearly.

But seeing.

And in a world as broken as this one?

That's a miracle.

I don't claim to be wise. Or whole. Or fixed.

But I do know this:

I'm not blind anymore.

Not to beauty.

Not to pain.

Not to God.

And that's what grace did.

Not by removing the darkness.

But by helping me keep my eyes open through it.

Part 5: Reflection and Scripture Integration

The greatest miracle wasn't that I survived Afghanistan.

It wasn't that I came home, or that Cathy stayed, or that my kids still crawled into my lap.

The greatest miracle is *perspective.*

I *see all of it now.*

Not through the lens of trauma.

Not through the fog of shame.

But through the quiet clarity of grace.

It didn't change the facts of my story.

But it changed the *frame.*

Grace didn't fix me. It just helped me stop hiding from the truth long enough to notice what was still good, what was still sacred, what had never actually left.

And now?

I notice things.

The laughter of my children during a moment I might've once missed.

The way Cathy hums when she wipes down the kitchen counters after dinner.

The wrinkled face of an old man at Mass, kneeling with tired knees and a look in his eyes that says, *I've seen things too.*

This is what grace does.

It opens your eyes to what's always been there.

The beauty.

The pain.

The people.

The purpose.

You don't need a mountaintop moment to know God is present.

Sometimes, He's just in the ordinary things you finally notice again.

The Scriptures have always known this truth. Isaiah writes:

"I will lead the blind by ways they have not known, along unfamiliar paths I will guide them... and turn the darkness into light before them."
...Isaiah 42:16

I know what it feels like to walk blind.

I also know what it feels like to have your sight restored...not in a flash, but slowly, like waking from a long sleep.

2 Kings 6:17 captures that shift too, when Elisha prays for his servant's eyes to be opened...not so he could escape, but so he could *see what was already surrounding him.*

"Open his eyes, Lord, so that he may see."

That's been my prayer lately.

Not for easier days.

Not even for complete healing.

But just this:

Open my eyes, Lord. Let me see what's holy in what I used to call ordinary.

Because when I see clearly...even through scars...I don't need every answer.

I just need to keep looking.

Reflection Hook for the Reader

Let me ask you:

What parts of your life have you been numb to?

Where has grace begun to shift your perspective...even if your situation hasn't changed?

What if the first step in your healing isn't doing more, but simply seeing more?

This isn't about hustle.

It's about vision.

And maybe...just maybe...that vision is the beginning of resurrection.

Part 1: Sharing a Story You'd Never Told

It happened in a coffee shop.

Not a pulpit. Not a conference. Not a planned support group with an agenda and a whiteboard.

Just two men, two coffees (in my case a Monster Energy Drink), and a conversation that wasn't supposed to go that deep.

He had just come back from a rough deployment...one of those where everything technically went "fine," but he was unraveling from the inside. He told me he couldn't sleep. That he couldn't sit with his family at dinner without staring off. That some nights, he drove around just to avoid going home.

I listened, nodding, letting him spill. I had no advice. Just presence.

And then...without thinking, without planning...I told him about the time I almost lost it during fireworks on the Fourth of July. I told him how I flinched at the sound of the dryer thudding unevenly. How I had disappeared behind my own eyes for months and didn't know how to explain it to anyone.

It wasn't rehearsed. It wasn't neat.

But it was true.

He looked at me for a long second. Blinked twice. Then said:
"Thank you. I thought I was the only one."

That moment lodged in me.

Because it wasn't just about what he needed to hear. It was about what I needed to say.

I had never told that part of my story to anyone who hadn't been *required* to know it.

Doctors. Chaplains. Therapists.

But this wasn't official.

This was *human.*

And for the first time, I realized: **my story wasn't a liability. It was a bridge.**

Not a bridge to healing all at once.

But a bridge out of isolation.

He didn't need my answers.

He needed to know I *had scars too.*

That he wasn't broken in a vacuum.

That someone else had walked through the darkness and didn't just survive...but stayed human.

That's what grace had been doing in me...not just saving my life, but repurposing the wreckage.

And in that quiet corner booth, I felt it again...not shame, not grief…

But *assignment.*

Not to fix.

Not to preach.

Just to *be there*...with truth.

That's the day I stopped hoarding my story.

Not because it was tidy. But because it was *true.*

And truth...when shared in love...is one of grace's sharpest tools.

Part 2: The Shift from Silence to Service

For a long time, I thought survival meant silence.

Keep your head down.

Don't stir up what you've buried.

Move forward.

But forward doesn't mean healed.

And silence doesn't mean peace.

In fact, silence had become a kind of prison. Comfortable in its routine, yes. Predictable in its numbness. But tight. Airless. Slowly choking the life out of me.

At first, I justified it: *Why tell this story? Who needs to hear more darkness?*

But over time, grace began to press in.

Not with guilt.

With invitation.

There was no trumpet blast or lightning bolt moment. Just small nudges...opportunities I hadn't planned for.

A young guy after church asking how I handled being home again.

Sharing perspective with someone who thought their world was coming to an end due to issues at work..

A stranger at a men's retreat who looked like I used to look...hollow-eyed and polite, waiting for someone to speak first.

Each time, I heard a whisper inside: *Tell a little more.*

Not everything.

Just what's needed.

And so I did.

Not because I was brave.

But because I started to believe grace doesn't heal us just for *us*.

It heals us to make us safe places for other people.

That's what service began to look like...not wearing a uniform again, not a new mission with badges or paychecks. Just showing up. Listening. Naming what I'd once hidden, so someone else could know they didn't have to stay hidden, too.

Grace doesn't demand that you be eloquent. Nor does it demand you search out an avenue to share your story.

It simply asks you to be *available*.

The cost of silence was that I carried everything alone.

The fruit of speaking?

It turned pain into purpose.

I wasn't trying to be inspiring.

I was just trying to be *useful*.

And maybe that's the beginning of real service...not when you perform strength, but when you offer weakness as a place of connection.

There's a verse that's become something of a quiet commission for me...*2 Corinthians 1:3–4*:

"[God] comforts us in all our troubles, so that we can comfort those in any trouble with the comfort we ourselves receive."

That's it.

That's the mission now.

To stop hiding the comfort I fought for.

To let someone else feel a little less crazy, a little less alone.

To stop believing my wounds were disqualifiers...and start believing they were a doorway.

And every time I choose to speak?

The silence loses a little more of its grip.

Part 3: You're Not the Answer...But You Can Be the Evidence

I used to think I had to *have something figured out* to speak up.

A plan. A platform. A clean ending. A nice, neat story

But I've learned this:

You don't have to be the answer.
You just have to be the evidence.

Evidence that pain doesn't have the final word.

Evidence that survival is possible.

Evidence that faith can flicker and still hold.

When people come to me now...veterans, church friends, struggling dads...it's almost never because I have a title or a job description.

It's because I've *bled.*

And I'm still standing.

That's what draws them.

Not strength.

Not speeches.

Just a shared ache...and the fact that I'm not hiding from it.

We think leadership requires certainty.

But the kind of leadership people actually need?

It looks more like presence.

It looks like a man who can say, *"Yeah. I've felt that too. And I'm still here."*

There's a quiet power in that.

Especially among men...especially those of us who were taught to armor up, to tough it out, to keep our stories clean.

But here's what I've seen, again and again:

Perfection isolates.
Pain...spoken with hope...invites.

When someone stands in front of me, hesitant, ashamed, half-speaking their truth and half-waiting for rejection, I've learned the most sacred thing I can do is not offer advice.

It's to *join them in the space they're afraid of.*

Not as a rescuer.

But as a witness.

"*I've been there too.*"

Just four words. That's often all it takes to build a bridge.

That's what Jesus did in *John 20*, when Thomas doubted. He didn't rebuke him. He didn't preach.

He said:

"Put your finger here. See my wounds."

Even the resurrected Christ still had *scars.*

That's not an accident.

That's the model.

God doesn't erase the wounds to prove He's victorious.

He shows them...to prove He's still human.

If that's how the Son of God leads, why should I be any different?

My scars may not be pretty. They're jagged, sometimes still tender.

But they're mine.

And when I show them, not for attention, not to impress...but to connect?

They become *evidence.*

Evidence that grace doesn't skip the pain.

It redeems it.

So let me ask you:

Reflection Hook for the Reader

What scars have you been hiding, instead of offering?

Who might need to hear your story...not perfectly, but honestly?

What if the very thing you thought disqualified you… is what God wants to use?

Don't wait to feel ready.

Don't wait until the pain is polished.

Just open your hands.

And let grace do what it's always done:

Take what's broken.
And make it holy.

Part 1: The Message That Broke the Fence

I honestly don't remember what I was doing or even where I was but I do remember that I looked around at the guys, and it just came out:

"The devil owns the fence."

There was a pause. Some nervous chuckles. But not from everyone.

Most of them just stared back. Still. Silent.

Because they knew what I meant.

They'd lived there.

We all had.

The fence wasn't between heaven and hell. It wasn't a moral scoreboard. It was that space in between, that subtle spiritual limbo where you're not doing anything "wrong," but you're also not really alive. It was the false safety of indecision, of waiting to feel "ready," of calling neutrality wisdom when it was really just fear.

I'd lived on that fence for years.

I'd gone to Mass, sure. I loved my family. I served my country. I even believed in God.

But I wasn't all in.

Not with my heart. Not with my scars. Not with my mission.

I kept one foot in and one foot out...telling myself I was doing my best, telling myself I was just trying to survive, telling myself grace would understand.

And grace did understand.

But it didn't excuse.

It didn't come to pet my fear.
It came to set it on fire.

When I said it out loud that night...**"The devil owns the fence"**...it felt like truth and confrontation all at once. Not toward the men in the room. Toward myself.

Because what I realized in that moment was this: the fence is not neutral ground. It's enemy territory dressed up as a safe option.

It's the lie that you have more time.
That someone else will answer the call.
That you can coast your way into sainthood.

But grace doesn't drift.
It doesn't hover.

It moves. It burns. It breaks chains.

And it's calling you off the fence.

That night, something shifted. Not just in me, but in the room. Afterward, one of the guys came up to me, quiet and red-eyed. He shook my hand and said, "Thanks. I've been on that fence for years. I think I'm done."

And I nodded, not because I had anything wise to add...but because I knew exactly what he meant.

You don't have to be a mess to be on the fence.
You just have to be waiting when God is already calling.

This chapter isn't a finger-point.
It's a flare.

Because I've lived too long with my soul half-awake.

And I'm telling you what grace told me:

The fence isn't safe.
The fence is on fire.
And it's time to get off.

Part 2: The Illusion of "In-Between"

There's a particular kind of spiritual anesthesia that's harder to wake from than sin.

It's not rebellion.
It's not unbelief.
It's apathy dressed in spiritual language.

That's where I lived for a long time. And honestly? It looked pretty decent on the outside. I showed up to church. I prayed sometimes. I was polite, paid my taxes, loved my kids, stayed faithful to my wife. I didn't curse loudly or drink too much. I was a good guy.

But I wasn't burning.

I wasn't alive.

There's a line in Revelation that used to make me roll my eyes...it sounded so black-and-white: *"You are neither hot nor cold. So because you are lukewarm, I will spit you out of my mouth."*

But once you've tasted the fire of grace...once you've known what it is to be awake...you start to see how terrifying "lukewarm" really is.

Because it masquerades as maturity.
It feels like balance.
It sounds like wisdom.

But it's nothing more than being spiritually undecided.

I didn't need rescuing from some visible disaster. I needed to be shaken out of my spiritual drift.

And that's exactly what grace did.

Not with lightning. Not with fire from heaven. But with something much harder to ignore: quiet dissatisfaction.

It started with noticing how mechanical my prayers had become. How I could receive the Eucharist and be thinking about grocery lists. How I could say "I'm fine" when my heart felt bored, confused, and cold.

And yet I kept walking that fence line, believing I was safer there than committing either way. I wasn't running from God...but I wasn't running to Him either. I was delaying. Numbing. Waiting for something dramatic to push me one direction or another.

Here's the truth: the fence seems like a safe place, but it's just a slow death.

Because it takes the urgency out of holiness.

It takes the awe out of grace.

It turns the burning heart of the Gospel into a calendar appointment you're already late for.

I remember a particular Sunday...years after deployment, years after starting to speak more publicly. I was kneeling in church, hands folded, face composed. But inside? I was flatlined.

No passion. No hunger. Just the empty ritual of religion without fire.

And right there, in that silence, I felt something deep within whisper...not in condemnation, but in truth:

"This isn't where I left you. And it's not where I want you to stay."

It wasn't about shame.

It was an invitation.

An invitation to stop surviving faith and start living it.

That's what the illusion of "in-between" steals from us: not our morality, but our mission. Not our salvation, but our surrender.

It teaches us how to look faithful without being faithful.

And eventually, if we're not careful, we learn to be okay with that.

So let me say this with the same honesty I needed someone to say to me:

The in-between is not where grace lives.
It's where grace waits.

But grace doesn't wait forever.

Part 3: Choosing Grace Means Choosing the Cross

There's a line we often skip over too quickly...Jesus saying, "If anyone would come after me, let him deny himself, take up his cross, and follow me."

We prefer our crosses decorative, not defining.

We put them on walls, around necks, on bumper stickers. But when grace really grabs hold of you...when it stops being a concept and starts becoming your fuel...it doesn't ask for decorations. It asks for surrender.

And surrender always costs.

There was a moment...a very real one...when I had to choose between comfort and obedience. Not in a life-or-death way. But in a slow-burning, identity-shaping way.

A man reached out to me once after a talk. A fellow veteran. His hands shook when he held his coffee. He didn't say much...just nodded when I spoke. But at one point, he looked up and asked, "How do you pray when you don't believe God's listening?"

And there it was.

The cost.

Not his question...mine. The cost was whether I would pretend to be strong and polished and "past all that," or whether I would admit, "Yeah. I've been there too."

I chose to tell the truth.

I shared about the times I'd sat in a chapel and stared at the crucifix without words. The nights I'd begged for sleep and got none. The mornings I knelt in Mass and felt nothing but fog.

I told him that grace didn't erase that struggle. But it taught me how to stay in it. How to bring the silence to God instead of walking away from Him.

That conversation didn't end with a miracle. It ended with a handshake and a quiet, "Thanks."

But something in me shifted that day.

Because choosing grace doesn't just mean receiving mercy...it means **bearing witness** to it. It means letting your life point to something other than comfort. Something bigger than safety.

It means choosing the Cross.

Not just the cross of pain or loss. The cross of **vulnerability**. The cross of obedience when it makes no sense. The cross of opening your wounds to someone else's so they know they're not alone.

That's the fire Jesus talked about...not the fire that destroys, but the one that purifies. The one that burns away the apathy and leaves only what's real.

Sometimes, choosing grace means choosing to forgive someone who never apologized.

Sometimes it means confessing a sin you've justified for too long.

Sometimes it means stepping into ministry you don't feel qualified for, because the Holy Spirit didn't ask for your résumé...He asked for your yes.

Let me be clear: grace doesn't bully. It doesn't coerce. But it will press.

It will call you deeper than you planned to go.

And it will ask for more than you thought you could give.

That's why grace and the Cross are always intertwined. Because grace isn't just sweet...it's **serious**. It's not just tender...it's **transforming**.

You can't carry both the cross and your comfort zone.

And grace...real grace...won't let you pretend otherwise.

Part 4: You Can't Stay on the Fence Anymore

There comes a moment when grace stops knocking and just waits.

Not out of impatience. Not because it's done with you. But because it has already extended the invitation...and now the ball is in your court.

I've learned something: the longer you sit on the fence, the more comfortable it feels. You start convincing yourself it's a strategic pause. A time of discernment. A season of waiting. But deep down, you know...it's fear. It's delay. It's disobedience dressed up as caution.

I lived that life.

There were years I went to Mass, raised good kids, stayed faithful in all the visible ways...but underneath, I was stalled. I knew God wanted more of me. More honesty. More risk. More surrender. But I kept hedging my bets.

I told myself I was "not ready." That I was "praying about it."

But I wasn't praying. I was procrastinating.

Because grace isn't ambiguous. It doesn't confuse. It doesn't whisper conflicting messages. Grace may not give you every detail...but it makes the direction clear. It points. It urges. It nudges.

And at some point, you realize the discomfort you feel isn't from not knowing what to do.

It's from **not doing it**.

There's a line I've said many times...sometimes to others, mostly to myself:

The devil owns the fence.

That in-between place where you're not rebelling, but you're not obeying either. You're not denying Christ, but you're not living like He's your King. You're not lost, but you've stopped moving.

The devil loves that place. Because there's no urgency. No action. No transformation. Just **spiritual drift** disguised as indecision.

You may be sitting on a fence of comfort. Or addiction. Or fear. Or control.

You may be on a fence that says, "I'll get serious when things calm down."

Or one that says, "I believe in God, but I'm not ready to change."

Or one that says, "I'm too broken to step forward."

But grace never leaves you there. It meets you on the fence. And then it points toward the fire.

The fire of commitment. Of mission. Of full surrender.

And here's what I've learned: **grace will not shame you off the fence. But it will not let you stay there either.**

Because the fence is killing you slowly.

You were not made to dangle between light and shadow. You were made to burn.

To step into the fire of purpose. To let the Spirit refine you...not because you're strong, but because you're His.

And here's the call:

What's your fence?

Is it the part of your story you won't share?

Is it the secret sin you won't surrender?

Is it the comfort you won't risk?

Is it the belief that grace is for everyone but you?

You already know the answer.

I did too.

And when I finally climbed off the fence and stepped into the fire...it didn't destroy me. It **refined** me.

It burned away what couldn't stay.

It lit up what had been waiting to live.

It made room for a life I never thought I'd be strong enough to live.

But it was never about strength.

It was about **yes**.

Part 5: Reflection and Call

This isn't a book about my life. Not really.

It's about yours.

My story just happens to be the canvas. But the brush is in your hand now. And the fire is lit at your feet.

Because if you've made it this far, grace has already found you. It's been circling you for years. Whispering when you were numb. Knocking when you were afraid. Holding when you collapsed. And now...it's calling you forward.

Not gently. Not sentimentally.

But urgently.

Because the world doesn't need more comfortable Christians.

It doesn't need more polished men who sit through Mass and never risk anything real.

It needs disciples.

It needs men and women who carry scars and still show up. Who still speak. Who still pray. Who are willing to be consumed by the flame of a mission bigger than themselves.

You were not saved to be safe.

You were not rescued just to recover.

You were not healed so you could return to normal.

You were made to burn.

And not with your own fire...but with the fire of grace that purifies, convicts, and sends.

So let me ask you plainly...because the time for subtlety has passed:

What part of your life is still sitting on the fence?

Is it your faith? Your marriage? Your silence? Your sin?

What is the fire you're avoiding because it might actually change you?

What would happen if you stopped treating grace like a guest and started treating it like your fuel?

You may never be fully ready.

You may still be hurting, limping, doubting.

But readiness was never the requirement.

Willingness is.

The fence may feel safer.

But the fire is where God is.

And He's not asking for perfection. He's asking for surrender.

He's asking for your yes.

So here's mine again...today, as I write this:

Yes, Lord. You can have it all.

The healed parts. The wounded ones. The ones still catching up.

I won't sit on the fence anymore.

I'm stepping in.

Part 1: A Quiet, Unanswered Moment

It was late. Everyone in the house had gone to bed.

The dishwasher hummed in the kitchen, and the dog had curled into that tight, warm coil at the foot of the couch. I stood at the doorway of my children's room...two sleeping lumps under mismatched covers...and listened to the hush that only a parent knows. That quiet where the breath of your child becomes sacred. That moment when your body is still, but your mind is anything but.

I watched them sleep...unaware, untouched, unburdened...and I whispered what I've whispered more times than I could count.

"Why me, Lord?"

Why did I come home, when others didn't? Why was I given this life...the second chance, the mercy, the years I thought I'd lost?

Why did You carry me when I couldn't pray, or speak, or believe?

Why did You stay?

And why does it still hurt?

There was no answer. No thunder. No voice from a whirlwind like Job got. No scroll descending from heaven. Just the rhythm of small breaths in the dark. Just the rustle of sheets. Just presence.

And maybe… that was the answer.

God didn't explain Himself.

He just didn't leave.

That was the miracle.

I used to think peace meant getting answers. That if I prayed hard enough, or healed deeply enough, I'd understand it all...the trauma, the timing, the deaths, the detours. I believed clarity was the reward for faithfulness. But I don't believe that anymore.

Because the clearest moment I've had in years was the night I realized I might never get the answers I wanted...yet somehow, I was no longer afraid.

Peace had come. Not as resolution. But as relationship.

Not as knowledge. But as nearness.

And in that moment, I didn't need God to explain. I just needed to know He was there. And He was.

He is.

This final chapter doesn't come with a thesis. There's no tidy conclusion here. No spiritual "aha!" moment to land the plane. What I've learned...what grace has taught me...is that we can be held even when we don't have a handle on everything.

We can be loved while still limping.

We can be carried even when the questions outweigh the answers.

We can stand in front of sleeping children, at gravesites, in churches, in boardrooms, or just over a sink full of dishes and whisper our doubts...and still be found.

Because grace isn't the end of the mystery. It's the beginning of communion.

And communion means you don't have to walk this road alone anymore.

Part 3: Faith Is Not Certainty. It's Communion

For a long time, I thought faith meant knowing. Knowing where God was. Knowing what He wanted. Knowing how the story would end, or why the hard chapters had to be written the way they were.

But the longer I've walked this road...the more I've wrestled, fallen, and limped forward...the more I've come to understand: **faith isn't certainty. It's communion.**

Some of the most faithful seasons of my life have also been the most silent. The driest. The loneliest. There were stretches where I sat in the back of Mass not feeling anything. Not joy. Not fire. Not clarity. Just... presence. And not even God's presence...just mine. Showing up. Staying put. Waiting.

And somehow, that was enough.

I used to envy the people who felt God everywhere. Who heard His voice in songs and sermons and sunsets. I don't envy them anymore. I've found a quieter miracle: **the grace to stay when nothing makes sense.** That's communion. That's love without proof. That's faith stripped down to its bare bones.

It reminds me of Peter. After many of Jesus' followers walked away...confused, offended, done...Jesus asked the Twelve if they wanted to leave, too. Peter didn't say, "We understand." He didn't say, "We're comfortable." He just said, *"Where else would we go?"* That wasn't clarity. That was commitment.

I get that now.

I think of Job, sitting in the ashes, covered in sores, asking God questions no man had ever dared to voice. When God finally answers, it's not with a neat explanation. It's with awe. With presence. With mystery too big for human language. And Job says, *"Surely I spoke of things I did not understand."*

I have, too.

I've tried to reason my way to peace. It doesn't work. Peace doesn't live in logic...it lives in relationship. In communion. In the daily act of turning your face toward God, even when you can't see Him clearly. Especially then.

There's an old phrase from the mystics...the "dark night of the soul." It's not depression. It's not despair. It's the holy ache of being held in silence. The kind of grace that strips you of answers but never lets go of your hand.

That's what I've come to believe.

Grace is not what I understand. It's Who I walk with.

And sometimes that walk looks more like a crawl. Sometimes it's quiet. Sometimes it's tear-stained. But it's real. And it's enough.

I don't need to know what's next. I just need to know He's here.

And He is.

Part 4: What I Can Say, After Everything

I've said a lot in this book. Stories I never thought I'd tell. Wounds I'd rather hide. Questions I still wrestle with. And while I don't have answers to everything, I've lived long enough...and survived honestly enough...to say a few things with confidence.

I don't know why I lived when others didn't. But I know I want to live in a way that honors them.

I don't know why the scars haven't all healed. But I know I'm no longer ashamed to carry them.

I don't know what God is doing most days. But I know He's not absent. And He's not cruel.

I've come to believe that grace isn't loud, but it's loyal. It's not always visible, but it's never indifferent. It doesn't erase the pain, but it never wastes it either. Grace has walked with me through war zones and hospital rooms, through therapy sessions and family dinners, through fireworks that made me flinch and Masses that made me weep. Grace stayed when I couldn't pray. Grace spoke when I couldn't form the words.

Grace didn't just pull me out...it taught me how to stay.

What I can say, after everything, is this:

You don't need all the answers to live a faithful life. You don't need to understand every part of your story to let it be used. You don't need to be whole to be willing. God isn't asking for polish. He's asking for presence.

So if you're reading this and you're tired, confused, haunted by the past or anxious about the future, I want to bless you with the same truth that's carried me:

May you learn to trust the silence.
May you learn to walk in mystery.
And may you never walk alone.

Grace isn't done with you. It never was.

And neither is your story.

Reflection Hook for the Reader

Before you close this book, sit with this:

What unanswered questions have kept you from peace?

Are there things you've been waiting to understand before you fully trust again? Before you pray again? Before you live fully again?

What would change if you began to walk with God before understanding everything?

Not walk ahead. Not walk away. But walk with.

Are you willing to trust grace, even when it's silent?

Because grace may not give you certainty...but it will give you communion.

Not every scar will fade. Not every answer will come. But the presence of God...the staying grace of Christ...that can be enough.

And maybe, just maybe, it already is.

Hey...

If you made it this far, thank you. Not just for reading...but for letting the pages sit with you.

I don't know what your story holds. I don't know what wounds you carry, or what you've seen, or what still wakes you up in the dark. But I do know this:

You're still here.
And that means grace still has work to do in you.

Not the kind that fixes everything in one prayer.
Not the kind that erases scars.
But the kind that walks with you. The kind that stays.

Maybe nothing changed as you read this. Maybe everything did.
Maybe grace just started whispering again.

Whatever the case...I want you to know you're not alone.
You're not disqualified.
You're not forgotten.
And you are not too far gone.

I wrote this book because grace wouldn't let me keep my story to myself. And if there's anything I've learned, it's this: the story that nearly broke you might be the one that breaks someone else free.

So speak it. Live it. Carry it well.

And when it gets heavy, let grace carry you.

A Blessing for the Road

May the Lord bless you with eyes that see what others miss.
May your scars become signs of hope to the wounded around you.
May grace meet you in silence and send you with fire.
And when the answers don't come...may you trust the One who does.

You're not alone.

Grace still holds.

Keep going.

...Ty

An Invitation to Go Deeper

This book wasn't written to impress...it was written to accompany. Whether you read it alone, in a circle of trusted friends, or with a small group, the real work of grace happens in what comes next: your own remembering, naming, and surrender.

Each chapter below is paired with a few prompts for prayer and reflection. Don't rush. Let the Holy Spirit guide the pace.

Chapter 1: Grace Opens Eyes We Didn't Know Were Closed

Summary: A quiet Easter moment stirred the memory of grace that had been there all along.

- What was your "Easter Mass" moment...the time you started to see again?
- Where were you blind to grace in your past? What do you see differently now?
- *Prayer Prompt*: "Lord, show me where you were...even when I didn't see you."

Chapter 2: The Song That Finds Us

Summary: "Amazing Grace" carries more than melody...it carries memory, mercy, and mission.

- What song or memory has God used to break through in your life?
- Have you let grace catch up with your story...or are you still running?
- *Journal Prompt*: "Grace sounds like ________."

Chapter 3: Why Am I Still Here?

Summary: Some men died. You lived. And the question never goes away.

- Have you asked "Why me?" What answer (or silence) did you receive?
- What grief still clings to your survival?
- *Prayer Prompt*: "Jesus, show me what you saved me for."

Chapter 4: Grace in the Fallout

Summary: PTSD didn't just affect the body...it disrupted the soul and the home.

- What wounds do you carry that are hard to name?
- Where has grace met you in your weakness?
- *Journal Prompt*: "This is how I feel when it's quiet: ________."

Chapter 5: The Cost of Coming Home

Summary: Some battles began after returning. Healing takes time...and grace.

- Who carried you when you couldn't carry yourself?
- What part of "home" has been hardest to reclaim?
- *Prayer Prompt*: "Lord, make my home a shelter of mercy."

Chapter 6: Grace in the Struggle to Stay

Summary: Marriage survived what war tried to destroy...but only through grace.

- What relationships in your life need grace to hold?

- Where are you trying to do things alone that need to be surrendered?
- *Journal Prompt*: "Staying has cost me ________, but it's given me ________."

Chapter 7: When Grace Looks Like Survival

Summary: Some days, grace looks like breath. Like not quitting. Like still being here.

- What's the "ordinary grace" you overlook?
- Have you honored the strength it took just to survive?
- *Prayer Prompt*: "Lord, I'm still here. Use that."

Chapter 8: Seeing Grace in Their Faces

Summary: The faces of the fallen teach us how to live. Their memory gives mission.

- Whose life (or death) shaped your own journey?
- What would it look like to honor them through your own life?
- *Journal Prompt*: "I carry ________ with me every day."

Chapter 9: Scars with a Mission

Summary: Grace doesn't erase scars. It sends them.

- Where are you still hiding your scars?
- Who could be helped by your honesty?
- *Prayer Prompt*: "Jesus, use what I wish had never happened."

Chapter 10: The Fence and the Fire

Summary: You can't stay neutral. Grace demands a choice.

- Where in your life are you still on the fence?

- What would it look like to say yes to God...completely?
- *Journal Prompt*: "What's holding me back from the fire?"

Chapter 11: What I Still Don't Know

Summary: Grace doesn't answer every question. But it holds us through them.

- What question have you been demanding answers to?
- Could you let that question become a doorway into trust?
- *Prayer Prompt*: "I don't know, Lord...but I trust You."

About the Author - **Dr. Ty H. Wenglar**

Dr. Ty Wenglar is a Catholic convert, combat veteran, former construction executive, nonprofit founder, and leadership strategist whose life has been formed through obedience, suffering, and the relentless pursuit of purpose. His message is not merely professional…it's personal, forged in seasons of disillusionment, refinement, and the unshakable conviction that true faith must move.

Ty holds a Ph.D. in Organizational Leadership and is the founder of Lucentra Advisors, a purpose-alignment consultancy that helps leaders and organizations root their vision in something deeper than performance. Over the past 25 years…first as an executive, then as a trusted advisor…he has partnered with corporate leaders, faith-based nonprofits, and mission-driven teams to close the gap between belief and action, between what we claim to value and what we actually build.

His credibility, however, flows not from titles, but from tension. As a U.S. Army combat medic in Afghanistan, Ty returned home physically whole yet spiritually unmoored. Years later, a mission trip to Rwanda became a crucible moment…where the contrast between war-scarred despair and dignity-rooted hope rekindled his faith, led him to step off the fence toward the Church, and revealed a deeper surrender that redefined his understanding of vocation. That same experience led to the founding of *Empowerment Through Entrepreneurship* (ETE), a nonprofit equipping women and small business owners in underserved communities with tools for sustainable, dignity-centered enterprise.

A life-threatening health crisis marked a second inflection point. Ty stepped away from a successful executive role in construction…not because he failed, but because success alone was no longer enough. He committed himself to helping others build ventures grounded in impact, integrity, and authentic human flourishing.

Through Lucentra, Ty now partners with leaders to align vision with values, cultivate cultures of clarity and trust, and pursue growth that serves both people and purpose. He is also a Certified Religious Freedom Consultant through the U.S. Institute of Diplomacy and Human Rights and a frequent speaker on leadership, spiritual clarity, and what he calls "post-comfort discipleship."

Ty has self-published three leadership works…*The Golden Rule in Leadership*, *Aligning Purpose*, and *Adaptive Leadership*…which Lucentra uses in executive roundtables, and mission-driven development programs. *The Devil Owns the Fence* is his first explicitly spiritual work…written as a bridge between formation and function, belief and becoming, faith and follow-through.

He is currently working on a second project centered on the grace of our Lord…not a theological treatise, but a heartfelt conversation between everyday Catholics and Christians. It reflects the grace he has experienced, continues to witness, and believes others are invited to see and savor as well.

He lives in Bee Cave, Texas, with his wife Cathy and their children. Together, they serve at St. John Neumann Catholic Church in Austin, where they're involved in engaged couples ministry and parish leadership formation.

This book is not just Ty's message. It's his story…and an invitation to step into yours.

www.ingramcontent.com/pod-product-compliance
Lightning Source LLC
LaVergne TN
LVHW100319210926
848480LV00003B/1180